AMERICAN F(

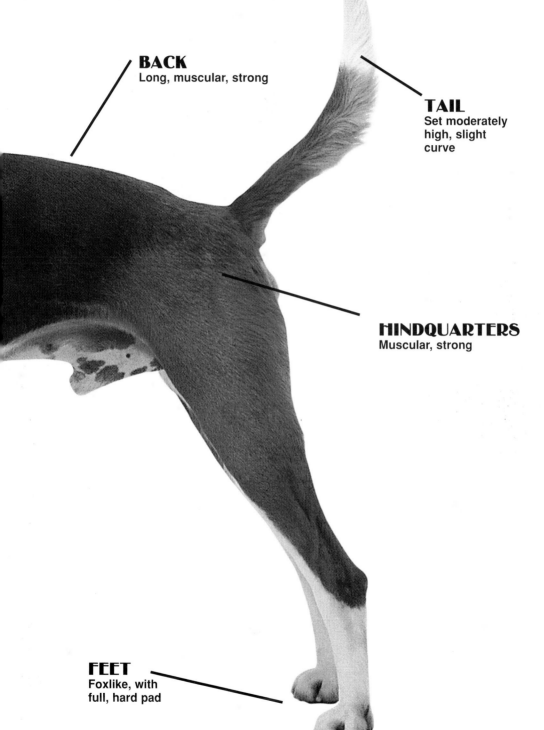

BACK
Long, muscular, strong

TAIL
Set moderately
high, slight
curve

HINDQUARTERS
Muscular, strong

FEET
Foxlike, with
full, hard pad

Title page: American Foxhound photographed by Robert Pearcy.

Photographers: John L. Ashbey, Bert Cobb, Isabelle Francais, E. H. Frank, Earl Graham, Patricia Haines, Julie and Ron Lux, John Miller, Johnny and Ned Moore, Robert Pearcy, Connie Petrick, Don Petrulis, Edd and Kay Phillips, D. B. Polk, Ritter Photo, Robert and Polly Smith, Buzz Taylor, Morry Twomey, George Vuilefroy

Acknowledgment
The authors sought and received assistance from far too many people than it would be possible to thank individually. A few do stand out, however, whose help was so vital as to preclude the possibility of not mentioning them by name. To Jo Ann Stone and the staff of *The Chase* magazine, we are truly indebted for all of the material made available to us; this book would not have been possible without their kindness. Cecil Boggs of Waynesboro, Virginia, was most generous and helpful in filling out our facts on the Trigg Hound. John D. Shaw of Walnut Hill, Illinois, shared much valuable information on the Goodman Hound. To these and to countless others, we are, indeed, grateful. At the same, we realize that no work is error-free, and the responsibility for whatever mistakes are to be found herein is ours alone.

© T.F.H. Publications, Inc.

Distributed in the UNITED STATES to the Pet Trade by T.F.H. Publications, Inc., 1 TFH Plaza, Neptune City, NJ 07753; on the Internet at www.tfh.com; in CANADA by Rolf C. Hagen Inc., 3225 Sartelon St., Montreal, Quebec H4R 1E8; Pet Trade by H & L Pet Supplies Inc., 27 Kingston Crescent, Kitchener, Ontario N2B 2T6; in ENGLAND by T.F.H. Publications, PO Box 74, Havant PO9 5TT; in AUSTRALIA AND THE SOUTH PACIFIC by T.F.H. (Australia), Pty. Ltd., Box 149, Brookvale 2100 N.S.W., Australia; in NEW ZEALAND by Brooklands Aquarium Ltd., 5 McGiven Drive, New Plymouth, RD1 New Zealand; in SOUTH AFRICA by Rolf C. Hagen S.A. (PTY.) LTD., P.O. Box 201199, Durban North 4016, South Africa; in JAPAN by T.F.H. Publications. Published by T.F.H. Publications, Inc.

MANUFACTURED IN THE
UNITED STATES OF AMERICA
BY T.F.H. PUBLICATIONS, INC.

AMERICAN FOXHOUND

A COMPLETE AND RELIABLE HANDBOOK

Robert and Polly Smith

RX-123

CONTENTS

INTRODUCTION

To undertake the production of an essay, an article, or a book on the American Foxhound is not only a daunting task, but it is also something of a presumptuous business. Deep-seated biases come out, even among our best people, when the hunters of Mr. Todd (Reynard) discuss the Foxhound.

There are wide ranges of style in hunting with the American Foxhound and much variation—with differences ranging between the English hunt style, the

Ch. Vaught's Hello Dolly, owned by Stuart Smith.

"forks of the creek" hunter, the Southern night hunter, the Northern hunter with a gun, and the field trial hunter. While it would be impossible in a small book like this to describe all of these with the differences in the type of hound required for each, we hope to cover the development of each to some extent. We must always bear in mind that foxhounds, like hunters themselves, come in all sizes, shapes, and colors. Some are lazy by nature, and all are lazy by design in the warm summer sun under the shade of a sturdy hickory or a spreading oak. Most (both men and hounds) are honest; some are dishonest. The dishonest hound is destroyed, so his corrupt genes will not be passed on to succeeding generations. As for the dishonest men, true hunters shun their company.

Emphasis in this book will be placed on four breeds or strains of American Foxhounds: the Walker Hound, the Trigg Hound, the Goodman Hound, and the July Hound. It is our hope that the reader will gain some insight, knowledge, and understanding of this native American hound.

As Mason Houghland wrote in 1933 in the foreword to his book, *Gone Away,* "Foxhunting is not merely a sport—and it is more nearly a passion than a game. It is a religion, a racial faith… an unconscious search for the eternal verities of fair play, loyalty and sympathetic accord…. It is a primitive faith, a 'survival'…. And it harks back to the clear and simple outlook of our tribal gods…. Like all religions, it has many sects. There are the very 'High Church' hunters with carefully observed ritual…. It is these Brahmans of the chase… (that) the world sees, the scarlet coats on green fields, the great leaps, the beautiful backgrounds (and even more beautiful horses)…. But … outnumbering them a hundred to one are the legions of foxhunters, like Franciscan Brothers, whose profession of faith neither poverty nor sacrifice can dim, some who must even deny themselves the necessities in order to keep a couple of hounds."

These words ring as true today as they did some 65 years ago, and they were true even earlier, in the latter part of the 19th century when the sport as we know it began to flower. Foxhunting brings together true hound and true hunter, whether mounted on the finest horse, driving a pickup truck, or following on foot. Money makes no difference to the true hound man. When the hound runs, all that matters to the hunter is the ability to breed and train an honest hound with heart, courage, stamina, and a good bottom.

THE HISTORY
OF THE AMERICAN
FOXHOUND

GEORGE WASHINGTON'S HOUNDS

While we know that there were hounds used for hunting the fox in the New World before those of our first president (after all, he got many of his hounds from Lord Fairfax), Washington's hounds were the first of which we have fairly good records. These hounds, descended

The American Foxhound is believed to be descended from foxhounds imported from Europe, like this English Foxhound. Photo courtesy of John Ashbey.

from English Foxhounds imported by Lord Fairfax and others, were comparatively "low and mouthy." These traits were well suited for use on the short-running grey fox, which was native to the Maryland/Virginia area.

Records show that foxhunting was a popular sport among the landed gentry of Maryland and Virginia as early as the first decades of the 18th century, but the most complete and detailed descriptions of the sport, the equipment, and the hounds come to us from George Washington's diaries. Known for his meticulous record keeping, Washington recorded for us not only details of the sport and its human and animal participants but the role the sport played in the colonies. Modern-day devotion to the sport in its many and varied forms is traced directly to those early times.

While Washington was famous as one of the preeminent horsemen of his era, he was first and foremost a hound man who managed his hound pack with the kind of personal attention not often seen in any time period. His records of the breeding, as well as the performance of his own hounds, were only part of the story. He also kept immaculate records of the packs of his friends and neighbors.

The fact that Washington's hounds were slow and mouthy was well established, but it was also true that they possessed good bottom and were fox killers. The same was true of other hunting dogs of that age and area. Indeed, it was good that the foxes available to them were of the gray variety, which was neither extremely clever nor far ranging. As is usually the case, this was a fine example of the game and the hounds being ideally suited to each other. As we shall see, the red fox, so popular even unto today, was not introduced to the southern colonies until near the end of Washington's life.

As noted, Washington's early pack was made up of English hounds. Interestingly, however, he did not import any hounds himself directly from England. On the contrary, he apparently preferred to build his pack primarily by purchasing hounds from the packs of his friends and judiciously breeding to the better males of their packs and raising his own.

One of his experiences with imported hounds is well documented. After the Revolutionary War, Washington found it necessary to rebuild his pack. A major contribution to this rebuilding effort was the gift of seven French foxhounds (three-and-a-half couple) from his friend and comrade-in-arms, the Marquis de La Fayette.

George Washington Parke Custis, grandson of the General, passed along an amusing story about one of these French hounds. At a large dinner party, Mrs. Washington noted that the ham was missing from the table. Upon inquiring of the butler, the lady learned that the hound, whose name was Vulcan, had invaded the kitchen, and, to the dismay of all the kitchen help, had made off with the ham. While Mrs. Washington was not amused, all the gentlemen had a good laugh at the incident.

Maryland hunters can be credited for introducing both the Irish Foxhound and the red fox to this country. This is an early gathering of American Foxhounds and hunstmen in Howard County, Maryland. Photo courtesy of the Howard County Historical Society.

THE MARYLAND HOUND

We can credit Maryland hunters for introducing both the red fox and the Irish Foxhound to this country. A print dated 1738 tells us that a group of planters in what is now Talbot County, on the Eastern Shore of Maryland, had a heated discussion on the relative merits of hunting the red fox as opposed to the gray fox. It seems that four of these planters had been in England where they hunted the red fox, and they cast aspersions on the ability of the gray fox to give a challenging and enjoyable hunt.

One of these planters, whose name has not been passed on to us, offered to have the captain of his tobacco boat, the *Monocacy*, bring back eight pairs of red fox on his next trip to England. This mission was accomplished. The foxes were turned loose in several parts of the county and soon began to multiply.

The winter of 1779-1780 was bitter cold, and the Chesapeake Bay was frozen over from November 1779 to April 1780. At this time, some of the red foxes crossed over from the eastern shore to the western shore. Over the next 20 years or so, the reds made their way into and began to spread through the counties of Hartford, Baltimore, Howard, Montgomery, and Carroll. These counties were preeminently the home of the red fox in its earliest years in this country. (There is a contrary theory that holds that the red fox was known in Canada and the upper part of the US. According to this theory, hunters from these areas gradually brought the red southward into Pennsylvania and Maryland, and it was from there that the red fox spread to other parts of the country. We find the first account more credible; the reader may make up his own mind.)

The above-named Maryland counties have a network of rivers and creeks cutting through the rocky bluffs, the banks of which were covered with ivy. Above the bluffs were thick stands of pine, and most of the river country was heavily wooded at that time. These rocky and vine-covered bluffs made an ideal home for the red fox, and they abounded with their dens. Where the red fox prospers and multiplies, the gray fox is inevitably pushed out.

Because the red fox ranges over a much larger geographical area than his gray cousin, and provides a longer and far more grueling race as a consequence, the local foxhunters were forced to change their ideas about what constituted a good foxhound. The indigenous hounds simply could not keep up with the red fox or stay the course with him.

In about 1812, a Maryland foxhunter named Bolton Jackson imported a pair of hounds from Ireland. These hounds, named "Mountain" and "Muse," changed Maryland foxhounds forever. From Mr. Jackson, they fell into the hands of Col. Sterrett Ridgely. In about 1822, these two hounds were given to Governor Ogle, who was so impressed by them that he bred them pure. From his resulting pack came the great hound, "Sophy." Old Mountain himself was eventually given to Mr. Carroll of Carrollton.

These Irish hounds, whose ancestors had hunted the red fox over very similar countryside in Ireland to

Foxhunters and a mixture of American and old Maryland hounds prepare for a meet of the Howard County Hunt during the 1800s. Photo courtesy of the Howard County Historical Society.

that in Howard, Baltimore, Montgomery, Hartford, and Carroll counties, had found a home in Maryland. The Marylanders hunted in the same way as their masters in Ireland had hunted. The ivy banks required a tough, wiry dog, and the long stretches from one river to the next demanded a hound with great endurance as well as speed. Most importantly, the Irish hounds also possessed great "fox sense" that enabled them to cast ahead when they lost the line, thereby gaining ground on the fox.

The Irish hounds had shrill, choppy notes; their ears were short, compared to the old gray hounds of the area. Their eyes were large, prominent, and dark, and they were dappled in color or flecked with bluish, gray-colored spots. They had heavy, rough, coarse coats that were of tremendous help in getting through the rough terrain in which they hunted.

Nearly every Maryland hunter crossed their hounds on the Irish foxhounds. Among the Maryland hunters who raised descendants of Mountain and Muse were the noted families of the Brookes and Griffiths of Montgomery County, the Hardeys and Linthicums of Howard County, and Nimrod Gosnell.

Mr. Roger Brookes, whose ancestor came to this country with Lord Baltimore, settled at the mouth of the Patuxent River, and brought with him his pack of English hounds, had the oldest pack of native hounds in Maryland. Among his pack was a most magnificent hound called "Brooke's Barney." Barney stood 26 inches at the shoulder, an immense size for that time, and was heavily coated with steel gray hair. His qualities were those of a first class hound: great speed and endurance, excellent carriage of head and tail, and a grand, earnest voice.

The painting "Full Cry" by 19th-century artist George Vuilefroy depicts foxhounds giving chase. They represented the qualities that hunters desired in a first-class hound: plenty of bone and muscle, great speed, and endurance. Picture courtesy of the American Kennel Club.

Opposite: The first American Foxhounds of the Virginia type had heavy, musical voices, long ears, and narrow chests. Drawing by Bert Cobb, courtesy of Robert and Polly Smith.

Nimrod Gosnell was a most painstaking breeder who could see the faults in his hounds and demanded the best to breed to the best. Mr. Gosnell bred and presented to Mr. Miles Harris of Georgia a pair of pups. The male of the pair was named "July," for the month he arrived in Georgia. July became famous in that country and was the progenitor of a strain of foxhounds that bears his name and that continues into the present day. July was instrumental also in the development of the Trigg strain of foxhounds. July was a medium-sized hound with a bushy tail, black back, ashy tan legs, and red sides.

Colonel Harris met Ben Robinson in November 1857 in Cincinnati while purchasing a carload of mules from him. The Colonel accepted an invitation to hunt with Mr. Robinson. Immediately after the hunt, he went by train from Cincinnati to Baltimore and on to Ellicott City in Howard County. He continued on by buggy about eight miles out of Ellicott City to Mr. Gosnell's house. It was at this time that Mr. Gosnell offered Colonel Harris a pair of hounds ("Tickler" and "Lade"). Harris did not wish to take advantage of his host and refused the offer. Instead, Mr. Gosnell arranged to breed the pair and send a pair of pups to his plantation in Georgia. Thus, Colonel Harris acquired the soon-to-be famous "July."

In Nimrod Gosnell's time, the Maryland hounds were of medium size. By the early 1900s, as the country in Howard and surrounding counties was cleared, the Maryland hound became larger and stronger. The open country requires a larger hound with a galloping stride.

The Maryland hounds bred down from Old Mountain are also found behind the Maupin-Walker strain. In 1867, Ben Robinson and General George Washington (Wash) Maupin ran a match race at Oil Springs in Clark County, Kentucky. The hunt was to be run on three successive days, and the rules were agreed upon. The Robinson hounds had more speed on the first day but were unable to go on the second day.

From that day forward, all friendly relations between the two camps were severed. Their breeding programs were punctuated by the same prejudice.

Maryland strains in Maupin-Walker pedigrees came from a hound called "Old Vick," owned by Jason Walker and by W. R. Fleming's "Bascombe" out of "Old Nan," both from Maryland. Robinson's Maryland hound, "Eagle," was the grandsire of Walker's "Old Nag" and "Moll," whelped in 1869.

George Washington Maupin, Tennessee Lead (the most famous hound in American Foxhound history), and William Jason Walker. Photo courtesy of the Chase Publishing Co.

THE MAUPIN HOUND

Daniel Maupin left his home in Albemarle County, Virginia and moved beyond the Alleghenies. The year was 1784, and Daniel went to claim the land that he was entitled to as a veteran of the American Revolution. He settled on land in what is known today as Madison County, Kentucky.

On December 10, 1807, a son was born to Daniel Maupin, and he was christened General George Washington Maupin after Daniel's famous commander-in-chief. George Washington Maupin (variously called "Wash" or "General" in later life) grew up to become the owner of extensive landholdings in central Kentucky and a plantation in Missouri. His Kentucky home was named "Hunter's Rest," and his main interest in life was fox-hunting. His favorite hunting preserve was over a thousand acres of land in Lincoln County. As he traveled trading mules and looking after his land, he became known as a great breeder of foxhounds. His hounds accompanied him on his travels, and he hunted with all the good packs of hounds he came across.

As Wash Maupin grew up, he had a close friend named Billy Walker, and the two were great hunting companions. Their friendship grew even stronger when Wash married Billy Walker's cousin, Mary.

When George Washington Maupin married Mary Walker, her sister married Wash's brother, Daniel. The Walker sisters were the daughters of James and Estelle Walker, who both died when the girls were young. Subsequently, the sisters were reared by a guardian who was a well-known hunter and hound man.

When Daniel Maupin moved, he brought his hounds with him from Virginia. These hounds were kept for chasing deer, and they also did very well on the native gray fox. Being of the old Virginia type, these hounds had heavy, musical voices, long ears, narrow chests,

Throughout the 1800s, many important hunters, like the Maupins, spared no expense in importing hounds from England in an effort to improve their breeding stock.

and rather indifferent feet and legs. They were slow and on the whole very sad looking. Their colors ranged from black and tan to mottled to red sided, black sided, and blue speckled. As noted, these hounds were very good on deer and gray fox. Deer were becoming scarce in the Maupins' part of Kentucky, and they had to go even deeper into the mountains to find them.

Washington Maupin had almost a national reputation for his hospitality and fondness for children, but most of all for being a great importer of the finest hounds to be found. He was also known for his ability to get the most out of his hounds and was able to make the sport of the chase into a profitable venture.

On November 20, 1852, a mule trader named Tom Harris gave Wash Maupin a rat-tailed, tight-haired, black-and-tan hound. This hound, which Wash Maupin carried across the pommel of his saddle as he stopped by his brother's home, became known as "Tennessee Lead."

Tom Harris "acquired" the hound when he was returning from Tennessee after taking his mules to market. Traveling by foot, he was intrigued when he heard hounds running. He raced to a crossing and caught the first hound. He tied the hound up and took him back home to Madison County, Kentucky.

At first, this hound turned out to be no better at hunting the gray fox and deer than other hounds owned by Wash Maupin, his brother, Jeff, and their neighbor, Neil Gooch. But one day a red fox crossed into Estill County. The gray foxhounds and deerhounds did not know how to cope with this new arrival. The Tennessee hound, Lead, jumped the red fox in the snow and ran him all day into a den on Round Mountain.

Tennessee Lead became famous for what was known as his "red-fox sense." Every hunter who had the means raised a litter of pups from him. Wash Maupin sent two sons back to Tennessee to get more hounds, but none turned out as well as the original. Tennessee Lead was of medium size, a black-and-tan hound with brown dots over each eye. He had a clear, short, rather yelping mouth.

General George Washington Maupin kept no records of his hound breeding. This was probably because Wash Maupin could neither read nor write. (As a bit of side history, it is interesting to note that when Wash Maupin died in 1868, his estate was valued at nearly one hundred thousand dollars—a tidy sum for that day, especially for a man who could not read or write.)

In 1857, a man named William Fleming came to Madison County and spent much time with Wash

Maupin, Jason Walker, and Neil Gooch. He brought hounds with him and when he left, he left two hounds behind—"Florence" with Gooch and "Vic" with Jason Walker. Wash Maupin must have been taken with Mr. Fleming, for he named his last child after him.

It was Mr. Fleming, an importer of fine merchandise from England, who suggested that the importation of some English hounds might solve the problem of the red fox. Consequently, on his next trip to England, he purchased two hounds and shipped them to William Jason Walker, Richmond, Madison County, Kentucky. The hounds were Rifler, a dog, and Marth, a bitch in whelp.

Every important hunter in Madison, Bourbon, Clark, and Gerrard Counties met the stagecoach bringing the two English Foxhounds from Cincinnati. Wasting no time in their anxiety to put the new arrivals to the test, a hunt was arranged for that very night. Marth was too heavy in whelp to hunt, but Rifler proved that he knew the ways of the red fox. Marth's pups all made good hounds and produced well, also. Marth was the better of the pair. She was bred to Tennessee Lead, but unfortunately, she died before the pups were born.

It should be pointed out that the Maupin hounds also carried Maryland hounds in their veins. Mr. Haiden Trigg wrote in his book in the early 1850s that the Maupins "imported many dogs from South Carolina, Virginia, and Maryland, sparing no expense to improve their stock." After the match race in 1867 between Ben Robinson's and Wash Maupin's hounds, tempers ran so hot that the Maupin-Walker group was reluctant to acknowledge the presence of the Robinson strain or any Maryland blood whatsoever in their hounds' pedigrees.

It was left to the Walker brothers and to three of Wash Maupin's nephews, Neil Gooch, W. C. Terrill, and Dan Terrill, along with his niece's husband, Arch Kavanaugh, to keep his memory and his hounds going. There is Maupin blood in both the Walker hound and the Trigg hound.

WALKER MEN AND WALKER HOUNDS

It seems fitting that the first Englishman (excluding those taken captive by Indians) to set foot on the soil of Kentucky would be named Walker. (This hunting trip was described by Joseph B. Thomas in his book *Hounds and Hunting.*)

Today, the Walker hound accounts for 90 percent of all registered American Foxhounds in this country.

Dr. Thomas Walker resided at Castle Hill in Albemarle County, Virginia. In 1742, he imported hounds from England to his home in Virginia. In the year 1749, he left Castle Hill with a hunting party to go over the mountains and into what is today Kentucky. Of course, he took his hounds with him, and other members of the hunting party took their hounds with them as well. On July 16, four months and seven days later, Dr. Walker returned to Castle Hill with the game he had killed: buffalo, elk, bear, deer, and turkeys, along with some small game. He also brought back wondrous tales of the beautiful, if forbidding, land beyond the mountains.

We move on from that time to 1785, when Asaph Walker married in Henrico County, Virginia and moved to Madison County, Kentucky. Among his many children, he had three sons named Stephen, William, and James. Stephen married and had one son by Mary Williams, who died very young.

After his mother's death, the child, John William (Billy) Walker, was reared by his mother's brother. Billy Walker was the father of the four Walker brothers who played a prominent role in the development and spread of what would become known as the Walker hound. These were Stephen, Edwin H., John Wade, and Arch K. Walker. Billy Walker was also Wash Maupin's friend and hunting companion.

William Walker was the father of William Jason Walker, who imported the English hounds, Rifler and Marth, in the fall of 1857. Jason's son, Colonel Charles Walker, and Jason's nephew, Richard White, first took hounds of this breed to Texas when they moved there after the Civil War. It was Texans who began calling this breed Walker hounds, instead of Maupin hounds. (It was Mary Walker and Nancy Walker, daughters of James Walker (son of Asaph), who married George Washington Maupin and his brother, Daniel.)

Within this family of men, most of the hounds to be known as Walker hounds were gathered. The original name for this breed was Maupin hounds. The history of the Maupin hound appears elsewhere in this work.

Wash Maupin did not keep written records of his breeding, and later breeders of Walker hounds must be very thankful for the records kept by W. S. (Stephen) Walker. He recorded everything in his private studbook and drove many miles to collect memories and records from other hunters. This Walker brother made duplicate copies by hand for his brother and his son. Through W. S. Walker's records, we find an unbroken line from Tennessee Lead, Neil Gooch's Old Aggie, Spotted Top, Scott, Blind Riley, and others to the Walker hounds of the present day.

In about 1845 or 1846, the first Kentucky hounds were shipped to market. They were bought by William Tisdale, a horse buyer from Tennessee, taken to New Orleans, and sold. By that time, there was a great market for trail hounds in and around New Orleans. The story was told that one of the hounds sold in New

W. S. Walker, one of the Walker brothers of Kentucky. Thanks to him, many American pedigrees from the early Maupin-Walker hounds were saved. Photo courtesy of the Chase Publishing Co.

Orleans returned to Kentucky within 14 days. (Whether true or not, the story is certainly believable. One of our Walker hounds—one that was blind—got loose a month after we moved from Michigan to Mississippi. He was home in three days.)

W. S. Walker made his first trip to Texas selling mules in the 1880s. He took four or five hounds with him, hunting as he went along. After his first trip, he took a larger number of hounds and fewer jacks to sell.

The characteristics that the Walkers most desired in their hounds were courage and gameness first and speed second. Rock, who won the first field trial, was a Walker or Maupin hound.

During the Civil War years, the breeding of foxhounds almost stopped. Most of the hunters of Madison County were in the roll call of Company E of the 11th Kentucky Cavalry. The company was formed by Robert Terrill, and all five of Wash Maupin's sons were in it, along with

Durret White and Arch Kavanaugh. After the war, the men who lived returned to Kentucky and resumed breeding the Maupin-Walker hounds.

By 1891, the Walker brothers felt that their hounds were too intensely inbred. This was the reason for the second English importation. Colonel J. P. Chinn of Harrodsburg, Kentucky, was an avid foxhunter and a friend of all the Walkers. While in Chicago, Chinn saved the life of a young Englishman. This young man obtained three hounds from his brother's kennel in Scotland. Legend has it that these hounds were smuggled out of England through the Pinkerton Detective Agency. The hounds came to New York in 1892 and spent six months in that city until found by an acquaintance of Dr. Chinn. This gentleman had the hounds shipped to Harrodsburg.

These hounds were Imp. (Imported) Striver, Imp. Relish, and Imp. Clare. These hounds had wonderful looks and carriage and added greatly to the beauty of the Walker hounds, particularly improving the feet. They were not any better in the field than what the Walkers already had. Striver was crossed on almost all the best bitches in this country. The Walkers got only four high-

Since the 1800s, Walker hounds have won every top field trial and bench show and are known the world over for their speed and desire to hunt. D. B. Polk with his Walker hounds circa 1949.

The Trigg hound, which has its own association and national specialty, is still very popular among hunters today. Trigg National Bench Show, 1999.

class hounds that they kept: Bragg, Mag, Big Strive, and Pearl Strive. When this outcross was made in 1892, it had been 30 years since the last outcross. The last of the old-line Walker stud hounds were Arp, Mont, and Blind Riley. Arp and Mont were both by E. H. Walker's Black Jac.

Today, the Walker hound accounts for over 90 percent of all the registered American Foxhounds in the country. Walker hounds have won every top field trial and bench show, as well as a number of AKC shows. They are known the world over for their speed and desire to hunt.

TRIGG HOUNDS

The Trigg hound, which has its own association, is still very popular among hunters today, second only to the Walker hound in popularity. While they are shown at the national bench shows and field trials, they have their own national specialty.

Mr. Haiden C. Trigg, the founder and developer of the strain of hounds that bears his name, wrote that from 1845 to 1860, his pack of hounds were the long-eared, rat-tailed, deep-toned, black-and-tan Virginia foxhounds. In 1860, the red fox made his appearance in the area around Glasgow, Kentucky, which was Mr. Trigg's home country. In 1866, Trigg began to correspond with Colonel

George L. F. Birdsong of Thomaston, Georgia, and in 1867, two years after the end of the Civil War, he purchased five hounds from Birdsong for a total price of four hundred dollars. These were Chase and Bee (by Longstreet), George, Rip, and Fannie.

When Trigg visited Birdsong a year later, he found the Colonel in poor health and able to take Trigg on only one hunt. Birdsong's pack, which still included the famous hound July (now ten years old), ran the red fox to ground in 45 minutes. Mr. Trigg wrote that, "By begging (for) two days and paying five hundred dollars, he let me have Lightfoot and Delta." A year later, on August 18, Colonel Birdsong died. At that time, Mr. Trigg had 14 pure Birdsong hounds in his pack.

Haiden Trigg was present at the famous match race between the hounds of Ben Robinson of Montgomery County, Kentucky, and General G. W. Maupin held in 1867 in Clark County, Kentucky. Trigg was among General Maupin's admirers and accompanied him home where they hunted for several days. On returning home, Trigg brought with him his latest purchase; a young bitch called "Minnie." On one side of Minnie's pedigree there were one or two crosses to Tennessee Lead; on the other side, she went back to Maupin's imported English hounds. He also brought home a young bitch named "Mattie," given to him by C. J. Walker.

Later, in 1869, Mr. Trigg visited W. L. Waddy and Thomas Ford of Shelby County. These gentlemen had pure Maupin hounds, and Trigg returned home with some of their best.

From 1867 to 1890, Haiden Trigg had the following pure strains in his kennels: 19 Maupin hounds, 14 Birdsong hounds, and 3 Walker hounds. He crossed these to his hounds to form his own strain, which became known as Trigg hounds. The fact that Trigg's base was in southern Kentucky, some distance from the Walker clan in central Kentucky (Madison and Garrard counties), allowed him to keep his separate identity.

Among the leading proponents of the Trigg strain in the early 1900s was Mr. Robert Rodes of Bowling Green, Kentucky. The hunters around Bowling Green are still today strong admirers of the Trigg. One of the best known proponents of the strain today is Mr. Ralph Hazelip of Bowling Green. Paul Rainey, the great explorer of Africa, was also an admirer of the strain, as was Mr. Joseph B. Thomas who used Trigg hounds to cross on his hounds.

GOODMAN HOUNDS

The famous Oil Springs match race in 1867 resulted in very strong feelings and great prejudice in the crossing of hounds owned by the participants in the match, as well as their adherents. The groups and their localities drew the lines and made their choices. Into this mix stepped Willis C. Goodman, originally of Albemarle County, Virginia. Mr. Goodman moved to Bourbon County, Kentucky, and added Maryland blood to the hounds he brought from Muddy Creek.

Mr. Goodman writes that Dr. W. E. Wyatt of Cyrena, Missouri, named the Goodman hounds "Goodman." Mr. Goodman gave some of his hounds to Captain R. L. Bowles of Palmyra, Missouri, and they made a very good reputation as red fox dogs. Other hounds of Goodman's breeding followed them to Missouri. Dr. Wyatt heard of them and wrote to Mr. Goodman seeking to purchase some hounds for himself. After Dr. Wyatt had tested them severely, he requested the liberty of using the Goodman name in a letter he intended to write to *American Field* magazine.

Mr. Goodman writes that the hounds he brought with him from Madison County were in "breeding, the same as the Maupin hounds." He felt that he had the "crème de la crème" of the Maupin blood, and he crossed these hounds on the very best of the Robertson or Maryland hounds. He was the first in Bourbon County to make this cross, and he had opposition from his fellow foxhunters.

The Goodman hound comes from Old Trix, Flirt, Lizzie, and Die, crossed on Wild Irishman, Tickler, Red Stag, Ben C., Whitey, and Fury, all of which were pure Robertson. This cross is the Goodman hound. Goodman emphatically stated that there was no Birdsong blood in them.

Mr. Goodman did not think that speed alone was the greatest requirement in a red fox hound. He wanted courage, speed, bottom, endurance, nose, fox sense, plenty of bone, and feet like iron. He wanted hounds that were able to hunt for five days and felt that the only fox hunters who put their hounds to as severe a test were the Walker brothers.

Goodman writes of selling a few hounds and of buying hounds from his hunting companions for hunters in other parts of the country. There is little doubt that it was this practice that gave rise to his reputation as a broker of or dealer in dogs.

In his book, *Fifty Years with Fox and Hounds* published in 1947, Mr. George J. Garrett writes very dismissively of Mr. Goodman. After calling him an old friend, he writes that Mr. Goodman was never a breeder of foxhounds, but was only a shipper of pups and trained hounds.

The authors find this allegation rather difficult to believe, as in 1894, he was a member of the National Foxhunters Association. He was on the committee of field trial foxhound breeders, named to draw up the first standard of the breed.

PENN-MARYDEL HOUNDS

In January 1934, a group of Masters of Foxhounds (MFH) incorporated the Penn-Marydel Foxhounds, creating a breed of foxhounds that had previously been shown in the American Foxhound classes. The organizer of this group was M. Roy Jackson, MFH of the Radnor Hunt. Among the packs represented in this organizing effort were the Rose Tree Hounds, Mr. Jeffords Hounds, the West Chester Hounds, the Pickering Hounds, Eagle Farms, the Huntingdon Valley Hounds, and the Rolling Rock Hounds.

These hounds were of the so-called "Eastern Shore" type (different from the Maryland-Virginia type). The Penn-Marydel hounds went back for generations in southeastern Pennsylvania, Delaware, and the eastern shore of Maryland.

The Penn-Marydel hounds were registered in the American Foxhound section of the *MFH Stud Book* and continue to be so registered today. In the registry, they are not distinguished from other American Foxhound strains.

The Penn-Marydel Association (the incorporators referred to above and their adherents) wished to create a new bench show classification. This appears to be why they incorporated and adopted their own standard.

In about 1946, after World War II, the Bryn Mawr Hound Show began offering classes for Penn-Marydel hounds, and these classes are still offered.

The question is often raised as to why two different types of foxhounds have evolved. The answer lies in the differences of the terrain over which the hounds are hunted. Southeastern Pennsylvania, Delaware, and the eastern shore of Maryland, over which the Penn-Marydel hounds hunted, is flat, open, and, for the most part, under constant cultivation. It is more

Two couples of Rose Tree Foxhounds, painted 1879-1880, represent the so-called "Eastern Shore" type of Foxhound, which was among the breeds that comprise the Penn-Marydel Hounds.

of a "cold-scenting" country with heavily wooded swamps. Hunters there needed a hound with good cold-trailing ability, and they wanted a majestic voice. This country is also intersected by waterways, so the hunters did not need a great deal of speed in their hounds.

THE FIRST NATIONAL

The first meeting of the National Foxhunters Association was held in November 1894, in Crab Orchard, Kentucky. The National Foxhunters Association ran the first National Field Trial in Bath County, Kentucky. The official record relates that because of dry weather, no decision was made. The reporters who were present were very considerate and wrote it up as just a Kentucky foxhunt, southern style.

In fact, the truth was that local hunters ran the grounds at night where the cast was to be made the next morning, because they held the affair in serious disfavor. There was so much opposition to this first National that hostile hunters burned some of the fields and created such confusion that a successful field trial could not be conducted.

The first American Foxhound to win Best in Show, Ch. Trix's Rex of Tri Van, owned by Mrs. Juanita Trisler, takes the title at the Panhandle Kennel Club Show in 1965.

John Fox, Jr., writing in *Scribner's* magazine, gave us the most complete description of the meet. It is a very good write up of the four Walker brothers and their hounds.

THE AMERICAN FOXHOUND CLUB

Although the Masters of Foxhounds Association was formed in 1909 by Harry W. Smith and a group that favored the American Foxhound, this group was soon outnumbered in the association by Masters who favored the English hound. The first stud book of the Masters of Foxhounds, published in 1909, was devoted to English Foxhounds. The South Lincoln Hound Show had even dropped classes for the American hound.

Opposite: Ch. Skyhill's Holly Kellie, winning the American Kennel Club Centennial Show under Judge Stanley Petter, Jr.

BEST OF
BREED

A.K.C. CENTENNIAL

RITTER PHOTO
BY KATHY

Thus, in 1912, Mr. J. B. Thomas issued a call to assemble at Burrland Hall in Middleburg, Virginia, to organize the American Foxhound Club (AFC). On March 9, 1912, nine gentlemen gathered with Mr. Thomas in Middleburg for this meeting. They elected David C. Sands, Jr. as the first president of the club. An executive committee was named, and Mr. Thomas was among its members.

A constitution was adopted, and it called for field trials and bench shows to be held. Although there was much discussion about field trials, none was ever held by this club. In 1935, and again in 1941 and 1945, the term "field trials" was dropped from the revised constitution.

Mr. Thomas, who was also a breeder and exhibitor of Borzois, had close ties with the American Kennel Club (AKC). In 1912, soon after its formation, the American Foxhound became a member club of the AKC. As a member club, the AFC was entitled to hold specialty shows. The inaugural bench show of the American Foxhound Club was held on February 15, 1913, at the North Avenue Casino in Baltimore, Maryland, under the rules of the AKC.

This club remained a member club of the AKC and the parent club for American Foxhounds until the early 1990s, at which time they resigned. By then, the club was run totally by members that hunted in packs and who had no interest in the American Kennel Club, at least as far as their foxhounds were concerned. Shortly before resigning from the AKC, the club changed its name to the Foxhound Club of North America.

In 1995, the current American Foxhound Club was formed, and most of its members were also members of the older club. The officers of the new club were Mr. Thad Haines of Ohio, President; Dr. Robert D. Smith of Virginia, Vice-President; and Mr. James Rea of Georgia, Secretary-Treasurer. Board members were Dr. Patricia Haines of Ohio, Mrs. Polly Dorsey Smith of Virginia, Mrs. Kay Phillips of Texas, Mrs. Judy Rea of Georgia, and Mrs. Ann Whitfield.

The new club was recognized by the American Kennel Club and held its first specialty show in Lexington, Kentucky, on August 31, 1997. The judge for the first specialty was Mr. Stanley "Hy" Petter of Lexington, Kentucky.

STANDARD FOR THE AMERICAN FOXHOUND

The first official standard for the American Foxhound was written on April 17, 1894, by Dr. A. C. Heffinger. The following men were also involved in the writing of the first American Foxhound standard: Col. Roger Williams, W. S. Walker, Francis J. Hagan, W. A. Wade, representing the Walker strain, H. C. Trigg, representing the Trigg hounds, and Willis C. Goodman, representing the Goodman strain. This standard was adopted by the Brunswick Fur Club on April 17, 1894.

Like all breed standards, the American Foxhound standard is a blueprint by which breeders can endeavor to create the ideal of the breed. Ch. Hazira's Dewey Brown, one of the top-winning, owner-handled foxhounds of all time, owned by Robert and Polly Smith.

STANDARD

Today's standard, which follows, is slightly different in matters of both size and feet. It no longer calls for cat feet as found on the English Foxhound. One point written in the first standard adopted by both The National Foxhunters' Association and Brunswick Fur Club is just as true today: The American hound should be smaller and lighter in bone than the English. The American Foxhound standard, like all standards, is a blueprint by which breeders can endeavor to create the ideal of the breed. One never quite manages this, but one can always dream.

The following is the current Official Standard for the American Foxhound.

Head—*Skull*—Should be fairly long, slightly domed at occiput, with cranium broad and full. *Ears*—Ears set on moderately low, long, reaching when drawn out nearly, if not quite, to the tip of the nose; fine in texture, fairly broad, with almost entire absence of erectile power—setting close to the head with the forward edge slightly inturning to the cheek—round at the tip. *Eyes*—Eyes large, set well apart—soft and houndlike—expression gentle and pleading; of a brown or hazel color. *Muzzle*—Muzzle of fair length—straight and square-cut—the stop moderately defined.

The American Foxhound has a fairly long and slightly domed head; moderately low-set long ears; large, soft eyes; and a straight, square-cut muzzle. Ch. Hazira's Billie Joe.

Ch. Skyhill's Holly Kellie winning Group First under judge and author Mrs. Polly D. Smith at the 1984 Southeast Missouri Kennel Club show.

Defects—A very flat skull, narrow across the top; excess of dome; eyes small, sharp and terrierlike, or prominent and protruding; muzzle long and snipy, cut away decidedly below the eyes, or very short. Roman-nosed, or upturned, giving a dish-face expression. Ears short, set on high, or with a tendency to rise above the point of origin.

Body—*Neck and Throat*—Neck rising free and light from the shoulders, strong in substance yet not loaded, of medium length. The throat clean and free from folds of skin, a slight wrinkle below the angle of the jaw, however, is allowable.

Defects—A thick, short, cloddy neck carried on a line with the top of the shoulders. Throat showing dewlap and folds of skin to a degree termed "throatiness."

Shoulders, Chest and Ribs—Shoulders sloping—clean, muscular, not heavy or loaded—conveying the idea of freedom of action with activity and strength. Chest should be deep for lung space, narrower in proportion to depth than the English hound—28 inches *(girth)* in a 23-inch hound being good. Well-sprung ribs—back ribs should extend well back—a three-inch flank allowing springiness.

Developed to hunt fox, the ideal American Foxhound possesses good muscle, stamina, speed, nose, and a grand earnest voice. Ch. Brown's Mr. Charger, owned by Ashlyn Cannon.

Ch. Kelly Mt. Prime's Lucky Lady winning Best of Breed at the 1998 Middleburg Kennel Club Show.

Back and Loins—Back moderately long, muscular and strong. Loins broad and slightly arched.

Defects—Very long or swayed or roached back. Flat, narrow loins.

Forelegs and Feet—**Forelegs**—Straight, with fair amount of bone. Pasterns short and straight.

37

Feet—Foxlike. Pad full and hard. Well-arched toes. Strong nails

Defects—Straight, upright shoulders, chest disproportionately wide or with lack of depth. Flat ribs. Out at elbow. Knees knuckled over forward, or bent backward. Forelegs crooked. Feet long, open or spreading.

Hips, Thighs, Hind Legs and Feet—Hips and thighs, strong and muscled, giving abundance of propelling power. Stifles strong and well let down. Hocks firm, symmetrical and moderately bent. Feet close and firm.

Defects—Cowhocks, or straight hocks. Lack of muscle and propelling power. Open feet.

Tail—Set moderately high; carried gaily, but not turned forward over the back; with slight curve; with very slight brush.

Defects—A long tail, Teapot curve or inclined forward from the root. Rat tail, entire absence of brush.

Coat—A close, hard, hound coat of medium length.

Defects—A short thin coat, or of a soft quality.

Height—Dogs should not be under 22 or over 25 inches. Bitches should not be under 21 or over 24 inches measured across the back at the point of the withers, the hound standing in a natural position with his feet well under him.

Color—Any color.

SCALE OF PONTS

Head	
Skull	5
Ears	5
Eyes	5
Muzzle	5
	20
Body	
Neck	5
Chest and shoulders	15
Back, loin and ribs	15
	35
Running Gear	
Forelegs	10
Hips, thighs and hind legs	10
Feet	15
	35
Coat and Tail	
Coat	5
Tail	5
	10
TOTAL	100

YOUR PUPPY'S NEW HOME

Before your American Foxhound puppy arrives at his new home, be sure to purchase the basic items he'll need and have a supply of the food he's been eating on hand. Ch. Winquest Deluxe All-American, owned by Julie and Ron Lux.

Before actually collecting your puppy, it is better that you purchase the basic items you will need in advance of the pup's arrival date. This allows you more opportunity to shop around and ensure you have exactly what you want rather than having to buy lesser quality in a hurry.

It is always better to collect the puppy as early in the day as possible. In most instances this will mean that the puppy has a few hours with your family before it is time to retire for his first night's sleep away from his former home.

If the breeder is local, then you may not need any form of box to place the puppy in when you bring him home. A member of the family can hold the pup in his lap—duly protected by some towels just in case the puppy becomes car sick! Be sure to advise the breeder at what time you hope to arrive for the puppy, as this will obviously influence the feeding of the pup that morning or afternoon. If you arrive early in the day, then they will likely only give the pup a light breakfast so as to reduce the risk of travel sickness.

If the trip will be of a few hours duration, you should take a travel crate with you. The crate will provide your pup with a safe place to lie down and rest during the trip. During the trip, the puppy will no doubt wish to relieve his bowels, so you will have to make a few stops. On a long journey you may need a rest yourself, and can take the opportunity to let the puppy get some fresh air. However, do not let the puppy walk where there may have been a lot of other dogs because he might pick up an infection. Also, if he relieves his bowels at such a time, do not just leave the feces where they were dropped. This is the height of irresponsibility. It has resulted in many public parks and other places actually banning dogs. You can purchase poop-scoops from your pet shop and should have them with you whenever you are taking the dog out where he might foul a public place.

Your journey home should be made as quickly as possible. If it is a hot day, be sure the car interior is amply supplied with fresh air. It should never be too hot or too cold for the puppy. The pup must never be placed where he might be subject to a draft. If the journey requires an overnight stop at a motel, be aware that other guests will not appreciate a puppy crying half the night. You must regard the puppy as a baby and comfort him so he does not cry for long periods. The worst thing you can do is to shout at or smack him. This will mean your relationship is off to a really bad start. You wouldn't smack a baby, and your puppy is still very much just this.

ON ARRIVING HOME

By the time you arrive home the puppy may be very tired, in which case he should be taken to his sleeping area and allowed to rest. Children should not be allowed to interfere with the pup when he is sleeping. If the pup is not tired, he can be allowed to investigate his new home—but always under your close supervision. After a

On his first night away from his mother and littermates, your little pup may miss their company. Giving him some extra attention will help him to overcome his loneliness.

short look around, the puppy will no doubt appreciate a light meal and a drink of water. Do not overfeed him at his first meal because he will be in an excited state and more likely to be sick.

Although it is an obvious temptation, you should not invite friends and neighbors around to see the new arrival until he has had at least 48 hours in which to settle down. Indeed, if you can delay this longer then do so, especially if the puppy is not fully vaccinated. At the very least, the visitors might introduce some local bacteria on their clothing that the puppy is not immune to. This aspect is always a risk when a pup has been moved some distance, so the fewer people the pup meets in the first week or so the better.

DANGERS IN THE HOME

Your home holds many potential dangers for a little mischievous puppy, so you must think about these in advance and be sure he is protected from them. The more obvious are as follows:

Open Fires. All open fires should be protected by a mesh screen guard so there is no danger of the pup being burned by spitting pieces of coal or wood.

Your home holds many potential dangers for a mischievous little American Foxhound puppy, like electrical wires that can be chewed, so think about these hazards in advance and make sure he is protected from them.

Electrical Wires. Puppies just love chewing on things, so be sure that all electrical appliances are neatly hidden from view and are not left plugged in when not in use. It is not sufficient simply to turn the plug switch to the off position—pull the plug from the socket.

Open Doors. A door would seem a pretty innocuous object, yet with a strong draft it could kill or injure a puppy easily if it is slammed shut. Always ensure there is no risk of this happening. It is most likely during warm weather when you have windows or outside doors open and a sudden gust of wind blows through.

Balconies. If you live in a high-rise building, obviously the pup must be protected from falling. Be sure he cannot get through any railings on your patio, balcony, or deck.

Ponds and Pools. A garden pond or a swimming pool is a very dangerous place for a little puppy to be near. Be sure it is well screened so there is no risk of the pup falling in. It takes barely a minute for a pup—or a child—to drown.

The Kitchen. While many puppies will be kept in the kitchen, at least while they are toddlers and not able to control their bowel movements, this is a room full of danger—especially while you are cooking. When cooking, keep the puppy in a play pen or in another room where he is safely out of harm's way. Alternatively, if you have a carry box or crate, put him in this so he can still see you but is well protected.

Be aware, when using washing machines, that more than one puppy has clambered in and decided to have a nap and received a wash instead! If you leave the washing machine door open and leave the room for any reason, then be sure to check inside the machine before you close the door and switch on.

Small Children. Toddlers and small children should never be left unsupervised with puppies. In spite of such advice it is amazing just how many people not only do this but also allow children to pull and maul pups. They should be taught from the outset that a puppy is not a plaything to be dragged about the home—and they should be promptly scolded if they disobey.

Children must be shown how to lift a puppy so it is safe. Failure by you to correctly educate your children about dogs could one day result in their getting a very nasty bite or scratch. When a puppy is lifted, his weight must always be supported. To lift the pup, first place your right hand under his chest. Next, secure the pup by using your left hand to hold his neck. Now you can lift him and bring him close to your chest. Never lift a pup by his ears and, while he can be lifted by the scruff of his neck where the fur is loose, there is no reason ever to do this, so don't.

Beyond the dangers already cited you may be able to think of other ones that are specific to your home—steep basement steps or the like. Go around your home and check out all potential problems—you'll be glad you did.

THE FIRST NIGHT

The first few nights a puppy spends away from his mother and littermates are quite traumatic for him. He will feel very lonely, maybe cold, and will certainly miss the heartbeat of his siblings when sleeping. To help overcome his loneliness it may help to place a clock next to his bed—one with a loud tick. This will in some way soothe him, as the clock ticks to a rhythm not dissimilar from a heartbeat. A cuddly toy may also help in the first few weeks. A dim nightlight may provide some comfort to the puppy, because his eyes will not yet be fully able to see in the dark. The puppy may want to leave his bed for a drink or to relieve himself.

If the pup does whimper in the night, there are two things you should not do. One is to get up and chastise him, because he will not understand why you are shouting at him; and the other is to rush to comfort him every time he cries because he will quickly realize that if he wants you to come running all he needs to do is to holler loud enough!

By all means give your puppy some extra attention on his first night, but after this quickly refrain from so doing. The pup will cry for a while but then settle down and go to sleep. Some pups are, of course, worse than others in this respect, so you must use balanced judgment in the matter. Many owners take their pups to bed with them, and there is certainly nothing wrong with this.

The pup will be no trouble in such cases. However, you should only do this if you intend to let this be a permanent arrangement, otherwise it is hardly fair to the puppy. If you have decided to have two puppies, then they will keep each other company and you will have few problems.

OTHER PETS

If you have other pets in the home then the puppy must be introduced to them under careful supervision. Puppies will get on just fine with any other pets—but you must make due allowance for the respective sizes of the pets concerned, and appreciate that your puppy has a rather playful nature. It would be very foolish to leave

It is important that everyone in the household learns to hold a fragile pup the proper way. Always lift your American Foxhound by placing one hand under his chest and the other under his hindquarters.

him with a young rabbit. The pup will want to play and might bite the bunny and get altogether too rough with it. Kittens are more able to defend themselves from overly cheeky pups, who will get a quick scratch if they overstep the mark. The adult cat could obviously give the pup a very bad scratch, though generally cats will jump clear of pups and watch them from a suitable vantage point. Eventually they will meet at ground level where the cat will quickly hiss and box a puppy's ears. The pup will soon learn to respect an adult cat; thereafter they will probably develop into great friends as the pup matures into an adult dog.

HOUSETRAINING

Undoubtedly, the first form of training your puppy will undergo is in respect to his toilet habits. To achieve this you can use either newspaper, or a large litter tray filled with soil or lined with newspaper. A puppy cannot control his bowels until he is a few months old, and not fully until he is an adult. Therefore you must anticipate his needs and be prepared for a few accidents. The prime times a pup will urinate and defecate are shortly after he wakes up from a sleep, shortly after he has eaten, and after he has been playing awhile. He will usually whimper and start searching the room for a suitable place. You must quickly pick him up and place him on the newspaper or

If you have other pets in the home, your new addition should be introduced to them under careful supervision. Rio and Rebel, owned by Connie Petrick.

in the litter tray. Hold him in position gently but firmly. He might jump out of the box without doing anything on the first one or two occasions, but if you simply repeat the procedure every time you think he wants to relieve himself then eventually he will get the message.

When he does defecate as required, give him plenty of praise, telling him what a good puppy he is. The litter tray or newspaper must, of course, be cleaned or replaced after each use—puppies do not like using a dirty toilet any more than you do. The pup's toilet can be placed near the kitchen door and as he gets older the tray can be placed outside while the door is open. The pup will then start to use it while he is outside. From that time on, it is easy to get the pup to use a given area of the yard.

Many breeders recommend the popular alternative of crate training. Upon bringing the pup home, introduce him to his crate. The open wire crate is the best choice, placed in a restricted, draft-free area of the home. Put the pup's Nylabone® and other favorite toys in the crate along with a wool blanket or other suitable bedding. The puppy's natural cleanliness instincts prohibit him from soiling in the place where he sleeps, his crate. The puppy should be allowed to go in and out of the open crate during the day, but he should sleep in the crate at the night and at other intervals during the day. Whenever the pup is taken out of his crate, he should be brought outside (or to his newspapers) to do his business. Never use the crate as a place of punishment. You will see how quickly your pup takes to his crate, considering it as his own safe haven from the big world around him.

BASIC TRAINING

Once your puppy has settled into your home and responds to his name, then you can begin his basic training. Before giving advice on how you should go about doing this, two important points should be made. You should train the puppy in isolation of any potential distractions, and you should keep all lessons very short. It is essential that you have the full attention of your puppy. This is not possible if there are other people about, or televisions and radios on, or other pets in the vicinity. Even when the pup has become a young adult, the maximum time you should allocate to a lesson is about 20 minutes. However, you can give the puppy more than one lesson a day, three being as many as are recommended, each well spaced apart.

Crate training is the easiest and fastest way to housetrain your American Foxhound. Crates are also useful when traveling with your canine companion.

Before beginning a lesson, always play a little game with the puppy so he is in an active state of mind and thus more receptive to the matter at hand. Likewise, always end a lesson with fun-time for the pup, and always—this is most important—end on a high note, praising the puppy. Let the lesson end when the pup has done as you require so he receives lots of fuss. This will really build his confidence.

COLLAR AND LEASH TRAINING

Training a puppy to his collar and leash is very easy. Place a collar on the puppy and, although he will initially try to bite at it, he will soon forget it, the more so if you play with him. You can leave the collar on for a few hours. Some people leave their dogs' collars on all of the time, others only when they are taking the dog out. If it is to be left on, purchase a narrow or round one so it does not mark the fur.

Once the puppy ignores his collar, you can then attach the leash to it and let the puppy pull it along behind him for a few minutes. However, if the pup starts to chew at the leash, simply hold it but keep it slack and let the pup go where he wants. The idea is to let him get the feel of the leash, but not get in the habit of chewing it. Repeat this a couple of times a day for two days and the pup will get used to the leash without thinking that it will restrain him—which you will not have attempted to do yet.

Teaching your American Foxhound good manners and obedience skills can help ensure that he will become a treasured member of the family for years to come.

Next, you can let the pup understand that the leash will restrict his movements. The first time he realizes this, he will pull and buck or just sit down. Immediately call the pup to you and give him lots of fuss. Never tug on the leash so the puppy is dragged along the floor, as this simply implants a negative thought in his mind.

THE EARLY DAYS

You will no doubt be given much advice on how to bring up your puppy. This will come from dog-owning friends, neighbors, and through articles and books you may read on the subject. Some of the advice will be sound, some will be nothing short of rubbish. What you should do above all else is to keep an open mind and let common sense prevail over prejudice and worn-out ideas that have been handed down over the centuries. There is no one way that is superior to all others, any more than there is one dog that is exactly a replica of another. Each is an individual and must always be regarded as such.

A dog never becomes disobedient, unruly, or a menace to society without the full consent of his owner. Your puppy may have many limitations, but the singular biggest limitation he is confronted with in so many instances is his owner's inability to understand his needs and how to cope with them.

IDENTIFICATION

It is a sad reflection on our society that the number of dogs and cats stolen every year runs into many thousands. To these can be added the number that get lost. If you do not want your cherished pet to be lost or stolen, then you should see that he is carrying a permanent identification number, as well as a temporary tag on his collar.

Permanent markings come in the form of tattoos placed either inside the pup's ear flap, or on the inner side of a pup's upper rear leg. The number given is then recorded with one of the national registration companies. Research laboratories will not purchase dogs carrying numbers as they realize these are clearly someone's pet and not abandoned animals. As a result, thieves will normally abandon dogs so marked and this at least gives the dog a chance to be taken to the police or the dog pound, where the number can be traced and

Training your American Foxhound is a learning process that requires time, patience, and dedication. This four-month-old pup has mastered basic obedience and has gone on to advanced training in order to compete in the show ring.

the dog reunited with his family. The only problem with this method at this time is that there are a number of registration bodies, so it is not always apparent which one the dog is registered with (as you provide the actual number). However, each registration body is aware of its competitors and will normally be happy to supply their addresses. Those holding the dog can check out which one you are with. It is not a perfect system, but until such is developed it's the best available.

Another permanent form of identification is the microchip, a computer chip that is no bigger than a grain of rice that is injected between the dog's shoulder blades. The dog feels no discomfort. The dog also receives a tag that says he is microchipped. If the dog is lost and picked up by the humane society, they can trace the owner by scanning the microchip. It is the safest form of identification.

A temporary tag takes the form of a metal or plastic disk large enough for you to place the dog's name and your phone number on it—maybe even your address as well. In virtually all places you will be required to obtain a license for your puppy. This may not become applicable until the pup is six months old, but it might apply regardless of his age. Much depends upon the state within a country, or the country itself, so check with your veterinarian if the breeder has not already advised you on this.

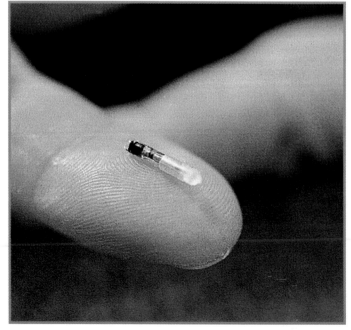

If your American Foxhound is lost or stolen, some form of identification can aid in his safe return. The newest and safest method used is the microchip, which is permanently injected into the dog's skin.

CARING FOR YOUR AMERICAN FOXHOUND

Before going into detail about the care of the American Foxhound, let me say they are easy to care for as long as you understand the nature of hounds. The American Foxhound has been bred over the years to be a fast, independent hound that enjoys the fields and woods. This is not to say that they don't make good pets—they do, but they require exercise and activities to keep their minds alert.

GROOMING

The American Foxhound has a short, double coat, which means that they shed. The foxhound will shed out in the spring, but he will also shed off and on throughout the year. They require weekly grooming. If they carry the proper coat, you only need to brush it. American Foxhounds do need to be bathed on occasion, certainly if they are going to live in the home, as they do carry a "hound" odor. Care needs to be taken that a hound does not constantly lie on concrete or other hard surfaces, which can cause unsightly calluses on their elbows.

When the foxhound is entered for shows, he does require some preparation for the ring. First, just as for a pet hound, he should be receiving a daily brushing with a hound glove. This takes the dead hair out and helps both the skin and hair to feel soft and maintain a healthy glow. Next, give the hound a bath using a good quality shampoo; never use a harsh soap on a hound. After bathing and drying the hound, use a hacksaw blade or trimming knife to clean up his neck and throat. You will also want to clean up the tuck-up of your hound with scissors. After you have done the toenails, which should

The American Foxhound has a short, hard, double coat that requires weekly grooming and an occasional bath.

Opposite: Bred to be a fast and independent hound that loves the fields and woods, the American Foxhound requires exercise and activities to keep his mind alert.

be done weekly, you will want to clean up the stray hairs around the pads. Removal of the whiskers is a matter of personal preference. If you are also hunting with your hound and showing him, I personally would not remove the whiskers. The stern should never be blunted or squared off, but left in a point. It is an insult to cut the tip of an American Foxhound tail.

The hair on the underside of the tail must not be trimmed, but may be combed against the grain to make the flag more prominent. This flag of hair is important to the hunters. It attracts the attention of the huntsman or field trialer, so he can see and locate the hound in the field. Often the only thing visible in deep cover is the white tip of the stern. This is one of the reasons that American Foxhounds must always carry their tail up when moving.

PHYSICAL CONDITIONING AND THE SHOW RING

An American Foxhound should be shown in good hunting weight. This does not mean that he should be skin and bones so that the ribs show, but he should certainly not be fat or in an overweight condition. The American Foxhound should always have good muscle tone. This requires daily conditioning—it cannot be done overnight. The American Foxhound is light on his feet and should display wonderful balance as he is gaited around the ring. The American Foxhound should move with his head out and in a smooth, flowing trot propelled by his powerful rear legs and fully muscled thighs. His front feet should reach out—never up as if he were a hackney pony. The American Foxhound is "stacked" or set up with a slight rise in the loin. One should remember that this rise is in the loin, not behind the shoulder. It should make a pleasant picture to look at. You want the American Foxhound to look happy in the ring with his stern up. Set your hound up with his front feet under him and his rear feet somewhat pulled back. Most foxhounds enjoy a piece of liver or chicken in the ring. It is wise to find something the foxhound is fond of and give that to him only in the ring.

NUTRITION

As far as nutrition is concerned, American Foxhounds will eat anything that does not eat them first. Good nutrition is imperative if you want your dog to develop properly. Dog owners today are fortunate in that they live in an age when considerable cash has been invested in the study of canine nutritional requirements. This means dog food manufacturers are very concerned about ensuring that their foods are of the best quality. The result of all of their studies, apart from the food itself, is that dog owners are bombarded with advertisements telling them why they must purchase a given brand. The number of products available to you is unlimited, so it is hardly surprising to find that dogs in general suffer from obesity and an excess of vitamins, rather than the reverse. Be sure to feed age-appropriate food—puppy food up to one year of age, adult food thereafter. Generally breeders recommend dry food supplemented by canned, if needed.

FACTORS AFFECTING NUTRITIONAL NEEDS

Activity Level. A dog that lives in a country environment and is able to exercise for long periods of the day will need more food than the same breed of dog living in an apartment and given little exercise.

Quality of the Food. Obviously the quality of food will affect the quantity required by a puppy. If the nutritional content of a food is low then the puppy will need more of it than if a better quality food was fed.

Your American Foxhound should have a healthy, well-balanced diet that includes the proper amount of proteins, fats, and carbohydrates.

Balance of Nutrients and Vitamins. Feeding a puppy the correct balance of nutrients is not easy because the average person is not able to measure out ratios of one to another, so it is a case of trying to see that nothing is in excess. However, only tests, or your veterinarian, can be the source of reliable advice.

Genetic and Biological Variation. Apart from all of the other considerations, it should be remembered that each puppy is an individual. His genetic makeup will influence not only his physical characteristics but also his metabolic efficiency. This being so, two pups from the same litter can vary quite a bit in the amount of food they need to perform the same function under the same conditions. If you consider the potential combinations of all of these factors then you will see that pups of a given breed could vary quite a bit in the amount of food they will need. Before discussing feeding quantities it is valuable to know at least a little about the composition of food and its role in the body.

55

AMOUNT TO FEED

The best way to determine dietary requirements is by observing the puppy's general health and physical appearance. If he is well covered with flesh, shows good bone development and muscle, and is an active alert puppy, then his diet is fine. A puppy will consume about twice as much as an adult (of the same breed). You should ask the breeder of your puppy to show you the amounts fed to their pups and this will be a good starting point.

The puppy should eat his meal in about five to seven minutes. Any leftover food can be discarded or placed into the refrigerator until the next meal (but be sure it is thawed fully if your fridge is very cold).

If the puppy quickly devours his meal and is clearly still hungry, then you are not giving him enough food. If he eats readily but then begins to pick at it, or walks away leaving a quantity, then you are probably giving him too much food. Adjust this at the next meal and you will quickly begin to appreciate what the correct amount is. If, over a number of weeks, the pup starts to look fat, then he is obviously overeating; the reverse is true if he starts to look thin compared with others of the same breed.

WHEN TO FEED

It really does not matter what times of the day the puppy is fed, as long as he receives the needed quantity of food. Puppies from 8 weeks to 12 or 16 weeks need 3 or 4 meals a day. Older puppies and adult dogs should be fed twice a day. What is most important is that the feeding times are reasonably regular. They can be tailored to fit in with your own timetable—for example, 7 a.m. and 6 p.m. The dog will then expect his meals at these times each day. Keeping regular feeding times and feeding set amounts will help you monitor your puppy's or dog's health. If a dog that's normally enthusiastic about mealtimes and eats readily suddenly shows a lack of interest in food, you'll know something's not right.

GENERAL MANAGEMENT

Proper nutrition and preventative health care are most important to seeing that your hound lives a long and happy life.

Make sure that your puppy has all of his shots. An adult hound should see a veterinarian once a year. Don't

It really doesn't matter what time of day you feed your American Foxhound as long as he receives the needed quantity of food. Older puppies and adult dogs should be fed twice daily.

depend on a hound to stop eating if he is sick. If your hound is only picking at his food or not eating at all, get him to the veterinarian at once. Parasite control is also much easier today with the use of different medications to control worms, fleas, and ticks. An American Foxhound that is given good care can live to 12 or 13 years of age.

The majority of American Foxhounds kept in this country are kept by hunters (field trialers, night hunters, hunt clubs, lone hunters, and deer hunters). The hounds are kept in packs, both large and small. Foxhounds enjoy the company of other foxhounds, and they are easier to keep if you have more than one. This book will not go into the management of hunting or field trial hounds, but rather the necessary care for keeping a few hounds.

The American Foxhound, from the early beginning, has been bred to hunt—and hunt he will. One must have a fenced-in area for American Foxhounds,

57

because they require a good deal of exercise for both their physical and mental well-being. If they do not get this exercise, they will get into trouble. If the American Foxhound gets free on his own, he will hunt, and this is one way you can lose him. He will come home; any good hound will find his way home if he is able (as long as he is not picked up, hit by a car, or experiences some other unhappy event). American Foxhounds are very intelligent—almost too intelligent. These hounds learn very quickly. Though their extreme independence prevents them from being popular in the obedience ring, they have been worked in obedience. One of the first foxhounds to be campaigned (in the late 1960s and early 1970s) achieved his obedience titles easily, but they will quickly become the clown in the ring, rather than the highest scoring dog.

Good nutrition and preventative health care are most important in ensuring that your hound lives a long and happy life. John Miller and his pal Ch. Kelly Mt. Prime's Lucky Lady.

SHOWING YOUR AMERICAN FOXHOUND

AMERICAN KENNEL CLUB SHOWS

The American Kennel Club (AKC) was formed on September 17, 1884, and two years later, the American Foxhound was admitted to their registry. At that time, the AKC had a Hound Group consisting of eight breeds. In *The AKC World of Purebred Dogs,* there is a list showing all registerable breeds, their country of origin, and the first dog of the breed registered. In the listing for the American Foxhound, the country of origin is cited as England/United States, the year 1886, and the first hound as Lady Stewart. Her registration number was 4320.

In Volume I of the *American Foxhound Stud Book,* published and kept by the National Foxhunters Association, Big Strive 41 (Champion under AKC rules); breeder-owner, Nowin T. Harris, Lyndon, Kentucky; black, white & tan D; whelped July 1893; by Imp. Striver out of Sal, by Bruce out of Dora, by Scott, etc., is listed on page 17.

When Mr. J. B. Thomas became president of the American Foxhound Club in 1915, he registered 48 hounds in the stud book of the American Kennel Club.

In 1894, the leaders of the Brunswick Fur Club and the National Foxhunters Association adopted The American Foxhound Type and Standard, drafted in 1893. The American Kennel Club subsequently adopted this standard.

In the early days of the AKC and on through the mid-century, American Foxhounds were reported shown in AKC shows, but never in large numbers. Then, in the early 1960s, a larger number of American

Foxhounds were seen at the shows. At that time, the AKC allowed "rare" breeds to combine sexes so as to make enough entries for the dog to get points toward his championship.

Among those showing their hounds at the AKC shows in the '60s were Dr. Fred Vaught, the Reverend Braxton B. Sawyer, Dr. Robert D. Smith, Mrs. Polly D. Smith, Mr. Johnny Moore, Mr. and Mrs. Truman Ashcraft, Mrs. Juanita Trisler, Mr. Jack Patterson, Mr. and Mrs. James Rice, Mr. Tommy Dunk, and Mr. Virgil Johnson, who at that time was already an AKC all-breed judge. Soon after, Mrs. Pat Kapplow began showing American Foxhounds along with her Bassets.

In the mid-60s, Mr. Buzz Taylor of Missouri bought a foxhound pup from the Smiths, and this hound became the first American Foxhound to win all the obedience titles offered by the AKC at that time. Ch. Buzz Taylor's Hazira's Foxie, CDX, UD, was an AKC conformation champion, won Best of Breed at Westminster in 1971, and was a Hound Group winner.

The original American Foxhound Club (AFC) did not offer specialty shows under AKC rules in the '60s. A

AKC Ch. Vaught's High Society and AKC Ch. Hazira's Samir were the first two foxhounds to become AKC champions in the state of Michigan; they are owned by Robert and Polly Smith.

number of the AKC exhibitors listed above joined, and Mrs. Polly Smith wrote the American Foxhound column in the *AKC Gazette* for several years. Although both Dr. Robert Smith and the Reverend Braxton Sawyer worked hard to bring the American Foxhound Club into closer cooperation and understanding with the AKC, nothing was accomplished. The American Foxhound Club continued to hold their bench shows separate from the AKC, and their shows were open only to American Foxhounds entered in registered packs.

Eventually, the original AFC resigned from the AKC. From that time, relations between the AKC and American Foxhound exhibitors improved, and today even more foxhounds are seen in the AKC show ring throughout the country.

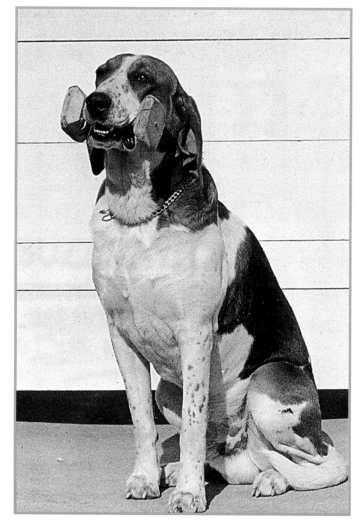

In the mid-'60s, Ch. Buzz Taylor's Hazira's Foxie, CDX, UD was the first American Foxhound to win all the obedience titles offered by the AKC at that time. Foxie also was an AKC conformation champion, won Best of Breed at Westminster in 1971, and was a Hound Group winner.

Ned Polk and Johnny Moore with their American Foxhound bench champions at an international show.

BENCH SHOWS

As stated in the hunting section, non-AKC American Foxhound bench shows are held, for the most part, in conjunction with field trials. These venues range from the National Field Trial and Bench Show to local county trials and shows. At all of these shows, the hounds that place on the bench (placings are from 1st through 10th) must be cast in the field trial to hold their winnings and must run until scratched by a judge.

In the 1960s, the Reverend Braxton Sawyer of Kentucky Lake Kennels fame and a number of other people got together and formed a new type of bench show—the International American Foxhound Show. There were no field trials in conjunction with these shows, but they were very popular and quickly became the benchmark for the show hounds in this country. They are still held every year. Among this type of show are the Royal, held in Missouri; the Florida International; the Virginia International; and the Georgia International.

In a sort of turn-around development, a new class has been added in recent years to these shows, namely, the running hound show. As the name implies, these classes are strictly for running hounds that have placed in, scored in, or won a field trial. This development has brought new hunters to the bench shows, and many of them have crossed their running hounds on show hounds.

The National Bench Show, held in conjunction with the National Field Trial, is held on the Sunday afternoon before the week of hunting. This show is judged a little differently from other bench shows in that there are only four classes offered. There are no classes for puppies at the National, so the four classes are Derby Dogs, Derby Bitches for hounds under two years of age, All-Age Dogs, and All-Age Bitches for all other adult hounds. After the four classes are completed, the two winners of the dog classes are judged against one another; likewise the winners of the two bitch classes are judged against each other. The winning dog and the winning bitch are then judged to pick the National Bench Champion for that year and the Best of Opposite Sex.

There are also special classes held at the National. One of these can be the Grand National Champion class. This class follows the judging of the regular national classes, and entries are limited to National Bench champions, including the one just selected. Obviously, if prior years' National Bench champions are not entered, this class is not held. Another special class is the Mason Houghland or "Natural Carriage"

Showing excellent conformation, Ch. Hazira's Cecil, owned by Robert and Polly Smith, wins Group First at the 1972 Beaumont Kennel Club show.

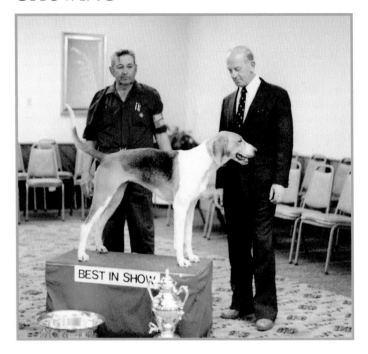

Ch. Brittenum's Jill, owned by Roger Brittenum, wins Best in Show at the Florida International Bench Show under author/judge Dr. Robert Smith.

class, open to hounds of either sex entered in the Derby or All-Age classes. In this class, the hounds are shown only on leash and not otherwise touched or handled in the ring. They are judged, as the name implies, on their natural showmanship. This class is optional at other affiliated shows.

Many but not all eastern, southern, and mid-western states have state associations that are affiliated with the National Foxhound Association and hold their own field trials and bench shows modeled after the National. These shows are open to hunters from any and all states. Likewise, most of the local county-level shows are affiliated with and run under National rules. Like the National, they do require the bench winners to be cast in order to hold their placings.

Puppies are shown at the international shows, like the Virginia International. The puppies do not compete for the championship of these shows. The puppy classes are held first in six classes: 0 to 6 months, 6 to 9 months, and 9 to 12 months, all divided by sex. The winners of the puppy dog classes are judged, then the winners of the puppy bitch classes. The two winners from this competition are judged to determine Best Puppy in Show.

The next classes are for the running hound show. These classes are judged in the same manner as the National, and a Best Running Hound in show and a Best of Opposite Sex are chosen.

After the puppy and running hound shows, the regular classes follow with the Derby and All-Age classes divided by sex. When the class enters the ring, the hounds are walked around for the judge, assisted by the ringmaster. The hounds are then placed one by one on the ten benches in the ring. At this, the judging—and the handling—really begin. The class winners are judged, and the winning dog and the winning bitch are judged for Best in Show and Best of Opposite Sex. There is only one championship awarded, which goes to the Best in Show hound. He or she becomes that show's International Champion for that year. We should note that bitches tend to win Best in Show as often as the dogs.

These bench shows are relaxed affairs, except for the handlers who are working very hard and with great skill to win the coveted spot.

Ch. Hazira's Bo Scott.

HUNTING WITH AMERICAN FOXHOUNDS

THE MATCH HUNT

English vs. American Foxhounds—November, 1905

This account is taken from Chapter II of the book, *Try Back: A Huntsman's Reminiscences,* by Henry Higginson and is the story of one of the earliest and most famous match races between the two breeds of foxhounds. The book was written in 1931, some 25 years after the match. Mr. Higginson writes his recollection of the match and what led up to it. His tale makes it clear that there was no love lost between himself and his fellow protagonist, Harry W. Smith.

Mr. Higginson was the Master of his own pack of English Foxhounds under the name of the Middlesex Hunt Club. Mr. Smith, of Worcester, Massachusetts, became a member of the Brunswick Fur Club (later called the Brunswick Foxhound Club) of Barre, Massachusetts, the members of which hunted in the traditional New England way. This style of hunting was quite different from either the English style of riding to the hounds (the style of hunting followed by Mr. Higginson) with a huntsman, whippers-in, etc. or the Southern style—also on horseback but much less formal than the English. It is important to note that neither the Englishman nor the Southerner would have considered shooting the fox.

The New England style of hunting involved a hunter that was on foot and armed with a rifle. He would loose his hounds (which were neither English hounds nor American but slow-hunting hounds) and take up a strategic position where the fox was likely to cross. The fox, not being pushed by the slow-moving hounds, ran in big circles, thus giving the hunter several shots at the fox. When Harry Smith joined the Brunswick Fur Club, it was comprised of quiet, old-fashioned New England sportsmen. Smith, who had hunted with Southerners, favored the faster and more competitive American hounds and wrote to this effect in letters published in *Rider and Driver.*

These letters were critical of the English hounds, a stance that Mr. Higginson disputed with vehemence. One thing led to another, resulting ultimately in an agreement to pit Higginson's Middlesex (English) hounds against the Grafton (American) hounds of the Piedmont Hunt in a match race to be run in Piedmont Valley, Virginia. The match would be judged by three men, one chosen by each of the two men and the third agreed upon by them.

American Foxhounds are used today by a number of hunt clubs. They are hunted in the same traditional manner as this pack of English Foxhounds, with hunters in formal dress and a Master of Hounds who makes all decisions regarding the hunt.

The men agreed to hunt on alternate days for two weeks, starting on the first day of November 1905. Under the agreed-upon rules, each party would hunt as many or as few couples of hounds as he saw fit, but they had to hunt the same number on each succeeding day as on the first.

Higginson selected 25 couples to take to Virginia and named 18-and-a-half couples as the number that would hunt each day. His hounds were hunted by a Mr. Cotesworth, and he used two whippers-in.

Mr. Smith hunted his own pack or, as Mr. Higginson called them, "his hounds," and surprised everyone by naming only six couples of hounds to be used during the match.

The match was held in Virginia, in the area of Loudoun and Fauquier counties. Mr. Higginson arrived at The Plains in Virginia, and stayed in Middleburg in the home of a Mrs. Brown, which the "Yankee party" had leased for three weeks. Mr. Smith and his party were housed in Upperville, Virginia. Mr. Higginson's judge stayed with the Higginson party, and Mr. Smith's judge stayed with him. The third judge divided his time between the two camps.

Though Higginson expressed his disappointment, the judges gave the award to Smith's American hounds. Mr. Higginson does note in his book that as he looked back on the fall of 1905, he believed that both he and Mr. Smith took the outcome of the match too seriously, but as he said, both men were young and "overenthusiastic." (Perhaps "hot-headed" would be a better word.) Higginson goes on to say that the relative value of the two breeds has been a never-ending topic of discussion. He points out that, as of 1931, the discussion had become less acrimonious. In fact, the discussion continues today among hunters and hunt clubs as to which hounds are better. Even within the world of American Foxhounds, among both night hunters and field trial hunters, there have been and continue to be heated discussions as to which strain of American Foxhound is best.

Opposite: Huntsman have long argued that the American Foxhound was faster and more competitive than the English Foxhound. The discussion continues today among hunters and hunt clubs as to which hounds are better. Ch. Hanfax Colorado Topez, owned by Juanita Troyer.

RIDING TO THE HOUNDS

American Foxhounds are used today by a number of hunt clubs. They are all hunted in the same manner, as are packs of English Foxhounds. The method of dress for the hunt is the same and there is a Master of Foxhounds (MFH) who makes all the decisions regarding the hunt. There is also a Huntsman who cares for, trains, and actually hunts the hounds, and he is assisted by one or more whippers-in. While the titles and terminology used in the sport are masculine, the positions described above can be and are filled by both men and women. *English Foxhound,* published by T.F.H. Publications, Inc., is a good reference to use for a more in-depth look at this formal type of hunting.

A tradition that is followed by the hunts and houndsmen is the Blessing of the Hounds. This is done every year in the fall at the opening of the hunting season. A priest gives a blessing to the hounds, the foxes, and the riders.

All hunting, whether formal hunts (live or drag), night hunting, or field trials, is done over ground through the courtesy of the landowners. It is customary to talk to the owners of the farms where your hounds will be running to let them know of your plans and to seek their permission to hunt over their property.

Foxhounds are taught or trained from an early age to ignore all farm animals or other dogs. (This perhaps is a good time to point out that a foxhound, whether American or English, is never referred to as a "dog"; he is always a hound.) It is important to foxhunters that a foxhound hunts the fox and *only* the fox. If a hound goes off on the trail of any other animal at any time during his training or while on a hunt, he is immediately pulled from the pack. If he can be placed with a deer hunter (in those states that allow deer hunting with dogs), that may be done. Often, the only recourse is to destroy the hound. While that may sound cruel, one can certainly understand that a hound hunting what the foxhunters call "trash" game will ruin the entire pack, as well as the sport for the hunters.

FIELD TRIALS

There are two "firsts" worthy of note regarding field trials held within the United States.

The first field trial ever held in Kentucky and most probably in the United States was held in 1864, and the prize was a silver collar with red plush lining and a lock with a secret spring. It was made in Baltimore and engraved as Billy Fleming ordered: *State of Kentucky, Madison County, The Fastest Foxhound in the State.*

"Bill Terrill's Rock" won the collar in 1864 and again in 1866. This trial was held annually for a few years, until feelings ran so high that it was abandoned (these were hard-riding and hard-drinking gentlemen).

The first field trial held in America for organized packs of hounds took place in November 1902 in Meadow Brook County in Long Island, New York. There were large sums of money wagered and a prize of one thousand dollars was offered for "the pack of seven couple of foxhounds showing the best field qualities." Judges for the hunt were Dorsey M. Williams, Master of the Patapsco Hunt in Maryland, and Harry Worcester Smith, who at that time was neither a Master or Huntsman of a

English-style hunting with American Foxhounds.

pack. Incidentally, this is the same Harry Worcester Smith who engaged three years later in the famous match with Mr. A. Henry Higginson.

Five packs of hounds competed: the Greenspring Valley Hunt (American), Meadow Brook (English), Aiken (American), Hickory Valley Hunt (American), and two packs entered by Mr. Herman B. Duryea.

After five days of hunting, a decision could not be reached. The judges felt that the Greenspring Valley and Aiken packs were so evenly matched in speed, endurance, driving, and pack work that the one thousand dollars was divided equally between them. Both packs were made up of American Foxhounds.

In Volume I of the *Foxhound Stud Book, National Foxhunters Association,* 1898, is a section titled "Running Rules and Regulations." In this section, they list their stakes and the order of their running: Derby for hounds under 18 months of age, All-Age for all ages, and the Champion Stakes open to all hounds that have won first, second, or third prize at any field trial recognized by the association.

Among the rules we found of interest were the following:

Rule 10: Riders to hounds shall be limited to the handlers with entries in that particular hunt, the judges, the MFH, the Flag Steward and members of the press who obtain permission from the Directors.

Rule 12: The Field Stewards, where practicable, should be sworn as deputy sheriffs...

Rule 14: There shall not be less than three or more than five judges who shall be elected by the Directors of the Club...

Rule 25: No hounds shall be eligible to compete in trials that have been hunted or kept within a radius of 15 miles of the meet within 3 months preceding the trials.

There were 26 rules and scoring was done with the following scale of points:

Hunting	.20
Trailing	.20
Speed	.20
Endurance	.20
Giving Tongue	.10
Judgment and Intelligence	.10
Total	**.100**

The rules for field trials today have been greatly expanded. A copy of the Rules and Regulations for Field Trials can be ordered from the National Foxhunters Association.

Because of the degree to which the country has been urbanized and built up, it is difficult to find the open land needed to hold the National Field Trial. There can be as many as 600 or more hounds in this trial. The hunt is run for three consecutive days for a minimum of five hours per day, unless called off earlier by the MFH. This is done if hounds cannot trail or run a fox, due to unfavorable conditions. All hounds are assigned a number, and this number is painted on each side of the hound by the owner.

The judges, all of whom are mounted so as to be able to keep up with the hounds, must synchronize their watches with that of the MFH each day. The judge must write down the exact time that he observed the hound at work and either scored or faulted him. The judges score the hounds in four categories: Hunting, Trailing, Endurance and Speed, and Drive. No one judge can assign a score to a hound—each recommends his score, and the score that the majority of the judges gave the hound is agreed upon.

Opposite: It is important to foxhunters that a foxhound hunts the fox and only the fox. If, at any time, the hound goes off on the trail of any other animal, he is immediately pulled from the pack.

Field trials are run early in the morning, with the hunters meeting at the kennels and being told at that time where the day's cast is to be made. The hunters then load their hounds (and horses, if riding), and the entire group leaves for the casting grounds. The hounds are lined up with their handlers holding their collars. At precisely 15 minutes after sunrise, the horn is blown, and the hounds are cast. The judges follow on horseback. The sound of the voices of 300 to 600 hounds being cast is truly unforgettable.

Two of the most prestigious field trials to win are the National and the US Open, but by far the most sought after win is the Chase Futurity, sponsored by *The Chase* magazine. The Chase Futurity marked its 79th running in 1999.

The Chase Futurity is run the same week as the National and on the same grounds. To be eligible for this event, hounds must be under two years of age and must, of course, be registered. The sire and dam, as well as the litter and the individual hound, all must be nominated

These hounds are numbered so that they can be scored in a three-day field trial.

beginning at the birth of the litter, and nominating fees must be paid periodically up to the Futurity itself.

At the National, as we noted earlier, the Bench Show is held on Sunday afternoon. The Chase Futurity is run on Monday, Tuesday, and Wednesday, followed by the running of the National All-Age Field Trial on Thursday, Friday, and Saturday.

For the winner of a field trial to receive a championship in the *International Foxhunters Stud Book,* there are a number of rules that must be followed. The field trial organization must be affiliated with the National Foxhunters Association, and the All-Age stakes must be run three days and under the National rules. The All-Age stake must have at least 50 entries, and the winner of the All-Age stake must score at least 100 total points.

The bench show must be in conjunction with the affiliated field trial and open to all—not just running hounds. The winning bench hound (Best in Show) must be run in the field trial and either be eliminated for a fault or finish the trial to qualify for the championship of that show and trial.

There is also a Dual Champion, which is that hound having the highest combined score on the bench and in the field. The dual championship has become an increasingly prestigious win in recent years.

A list of affiliated field trials (those run under National rules) run each year is found on the first page of *The Chase.* Field trials are hosted by breeds or strains, such as the Trigg National, by state associations, such as the Pennsylvania State Foxhunters Association, and by regional hunts, such as the South Mississippi Foxhunters Association. All of these trials must be run for three days. Other county associations and some regional hunts are held for one or two days. These also usually hold bench shows in conjunction with the field trials.

The records of the National Foxhunters Association and the registrations of the *International Foxhunters Stud Book* are kept in the office of the Chase Publishing Company, which publishes *The Chase. The Chase* and *The Hunters Horn* are the two magazines of record for foxhunters. *The Hunters Horn* publishes the *Standard Foxhound Stud Book* and lists upcoming hunts.

THE NIGHT HUNTERS

By far the majority of the foxhunters in this country are called variously the forks of the creek hunters, hilltoppers, or night hunters. These are the men (and a few women) who keep from 1 to 20 or so hounds for the pure joy of hearing a good race. Most of these men are dirt farmers, work in the coal mines of southwestern Virginia, West Virginia, and Kentucky, or work in the factories that dot the rural countryside. They are unable to hunt during the day or to keep large packs, but they are able to forego sleep and go to the fields, woods, and hills for a fox race from about 9:00 or 9:30 at night and stay out until the wee hours before daybreak. These are the men who keep the sport of foxhunting alive today.

FOX PENS AND DRAG HUNTS

A new type of hunting has come into being in the 1980s and 1990s. This is hunting in what are called "fox pens." Because of the great urban and suburban growth in the mid-Atlantic and Sun Belt regions, the foxhunters have found it even more difficult to find the open spaces that are required for the safety of both hounds and men when foxhunting. Consequently, they have gone to fox pens for the training and hunting of their hounds. These "pens" are large tracts of land that are fenced in to hold both the fox and the hounds. They can range from 100 acres to 1,000 acres and more. The pens have worked out as satisfactory training grounds, but even their most enthusiastic devotees would hardly claim that they really substitute for the real thing.

The formal hunts in many areas of the Northeast have gone to drag hunts as opposed to hunting live fox. In the drag hunt, a line or course is laid out by dragging the scent of the fox along a trail through the fields and woods. The line can be as long or as short as desired. Although drag hunting is not new (Mr. Higginson made reference to its occurrence at around the turn of the century), it has certainly become more popular today than it was in the past for the same reasons that fox pens have become popular with the night hunters.

These changes may not be satisfactory to all hunters, and purists may frown on them, but both for the safety of the hounds and for the continuation of the sport into the future, they are necessary. This is one more reason that good relationships between hunters and farmers are so important.

OTHER HUNTERS

Foxhounds are also hunted on game other than fox. Deer hunting with hounds has already been mentioned. Men who moved west came to areas where the fox was not so popular, so they trained their hounds on wolves

Foxhunting brings together true hound and true hunter, whether mounted on the finest horse, driving a pickup truck, or following on foot. Ch. Vaught's High Society.

and coyotes, and the hounds performed well on the larger game. It should be mentioned, however, that both the more open country and the larger game required these hunters to produce a larger hound. A number of hunters use the foxhound on such game as bobcat, cougar, and bear, and a few even use them on panthers in the swamps of the South.

We hope that this rather lengthy discourse on the various forms of hunting with the American Foxhound has given the reader a taste of the richness as well as the variety of the sport of hounds.

YOUR HEALTHY AMERICAN FOXHOUND

Dogs, like all other animals, are capable of contracting problems and diseases that, in most cases, are easily avoided by sound husbandry—meaning well-bred and well-cared-for animals are less prone to developing diseases and problems than are carelessly bred and neglected animals. Your knowledge of how to avoid problems is far more valuable than all of the books and advice on how to cure them. Respectively, the only person you should listen to about treatment is your vet. Veterinarians don't have all the answers, but at least they are trained to analyze and treat illnesses, and are aware of the full implications of treatments. This does not mean a few old remedies aren't good standbys when all else fails, but in most cases modern science provides the best treatments for disease.

Opposite: As a responsible American Foxhound owner, you should have a basic understanding of the medical problems that affect the breed.

PHYSICAL EXAMS

Your puppy should receive regular physical examinations or checkups. These come in two forms. One is obviously performed by your vet, and the other is a day-to-day procedure that should be done by you. Apart from the fact the exam will highlight any problem at an early stage, it is an excellent way of socializing the pup to being handled.

To do the physical exam yourself, start at the head and work your way around the body. You are looking for any sign of lesions, or any indication of parasites on the pup. The most common parasites are fleas and ticks.

HEALTHY TEETH AND GUMS

Chewing is instinctual. Puppies chew so that their teeth and jaws grow strong and healthy as they develop.

Healthy teeth and gums are important to the well-being of your American Foxhound. Check and brush his teeth regularly.

As the permanent teeth begin to emerge, it is painful and annoying to the puppy, and puppy owners must recognize that their new charges need something safe upon which to chew. Unfortunately, once the puppy's permanent teeth have emerged and settled solidly into the jaw, the chewing instinct does not fade. Adult dogs instinctively need to clean their teeth, massage their gums, and exercise their jaws through chewing.

It is necessary for your dog to have clean teeth. You should take your dog to the veterinarian at least once a year to have his teeth cleaned and to have his mouth examined for any sign of oral disease. Although dogs do not get cavities in the same way humans do, dogs' teeth accumulate tartar, and more quickly than humans do! Veterinarians recommend brushing your dog's teeth daily. But who can find time to brush their dog's teeth daily? The accumulation of tartar and plaque on our dog's teeth when not removed can cause irritation and eventually erode the enamel and finally destroy the teeth. Advanced cases, while destroying the teeth, bring on gingivitis and periodontitis, two very serious conditions that can affect the dog's internal organs as well...to say nothing about bad breath!

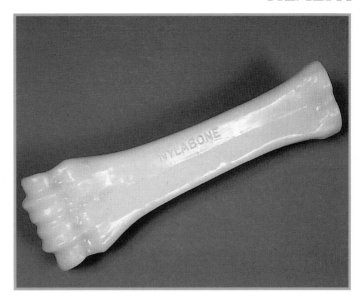

Chew toys not only keep your American Foxhounds teeth clean, but they also relieve stress and provide entertainment. Nylabone® is the only plastic dog bone made of 100 percent virgin nylon, specially processed to create a tough, durable, completely safe bone.

Since everyone can't brush their dog's teeth daily or get to the veterinarian often enough for him to scale the dog's teeth, providing the dog with something safe to chew on will help maintain oral hygeine. Chew devices from Nylabone® keep dogs' teeth clean, but they also provide an excellent resource for entertainment and relief of doggie tensions. Nylabone® products give your dog something to do for an hour or two every day and during that hour or two, your dog will be taking an active part in keeping his teeth and gums healthy...without even realizing it! That's invaluable to your dog, and valuable to you!

Nylabone® provides fun bones, challenging bones, and *safe* bones. It is an owner's responsibility to recognize safe chew toys from dangerous ones. Your dog will chew and devour anything you give him. Dogs must not be permitted to chew on items that they can break. Pieces of broken objects can do internal damage to a

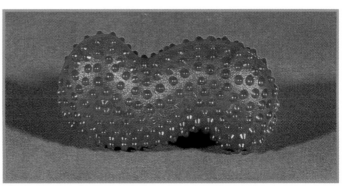

The Hercules® by Nylabone® has raised dental tips that help fight plaque on your hound's teeth.

dog, besides ripping the dog's mouth. Cheap plastic or rubber toys can cause stoppage in the intestines; such stoppages are operable only if caught immediately.

The most obvious choices, in this case, may be the worst choice. Natural beef bones were not designed for chewing and cannot take too much pressure from the sides. Due to the abrasive nature of these bones, they should be offered most sparingly. Knuckle bones, though once very popular for dogs, can be easily chewed up and eaten by dogs. At the very least, digestion is interrupted; at worst, the dog can choke or suffer from intestinal blockage.

When a dog chews hard on a Nylabone®, little bristle-like projections appear on the surface of the bone. These help to clean the dog's teeth and add to the gum-massaging. Given the chemistry of the nylon, the bristle can pass through the dog's intestinal tract without effect. Since nylon is inert, no microorganism can grow on it, and it can be washed in soap and water or sterilized in boiling water or in an autoclave.

For the sake of your dog, his teeth and your own peace of mind, provide your dog with Nylabones®. They have 100 varieties from which to choose.

FIGHTING FLEAS

Fleas are very mobile and may be red, black, or brown in color. The adults suck the blood of the host, while the larvae feed on the feces of the adults, which is

There are many parasites, like fleas and ticks, that your dog may encounter when playing outside. Be sure to check his coat thoroughly when he comes in from the outdoors.

The cat flea is the most common flea of dogs. It starts feeding soon after it makes contact with the dog.

rich in blood. Flea "dirt" may be seen on the pup as very tiny clusters of blackish specks that look like freshly ground pepper. The eggs of fleas may be laid on the puppy, though they are more commonly laid off the host in a favorable place, such as the bedding. They normally hatch in 4 to 21 days, depending on the temperature, but they can survive for up to 18 months if temperature conditions are not favorable. The larvae are maggot-like and molt a couple of times before forming pupae, which can survive long periods until the temperature, or the vibration of a nearby host, causes them to emerge and jump on a host.

There are a number of effective treatments available, and you should discuss them with your veterinarian, then follow all instructions for the one you choose. Any treatment will involve a product for your puppy or dog and one for the environment, and will require diligence on your part to treat all areas and thoroughly clean your home and yard until the infestation is eradicated.

THE TROUBLE WITH TICKS

Ticks are arthropods of the spider family, which means they have eight legs (though the larvae have six). They bury their headparts into the host and gorge on its blood. They are easily seen as small grain-like creatures sticking out from the skin. They are often picked up when dogs play in fields, but may also arrive in your yard via wild animals—even birds—or stray cats and dogs. Some ticks are species-specific, others are more adaptable and will host on many species.

The deer tick is the most common carrier of Lyme disease. Photo courtesy of Virbac Laboratories, Inc., Fort Worth, Texas.

The most troublesome type of tick is the deer tick, which spreads the deadly Lyme disease that can cripple a dog (or a person). Deer ticks are tiny and very hard to detect. Often, by the time they're big enough to notice, they've been feeding on the dog for a few days—long enough to do their damage. Lyme disease was named for the area of the United States in which it was first detected—Lyme, Connecticut—but has now been diagnosed in almost all parts of the US. Your veterinarian can advise you of the danger to your dog(s) in your area, and may suggest your dog be vaccinated for Lyme. Always go over your dog with a fine-toothed flea comb when you come in from walking through any area that may harbor deer ticks, and if your dog is acting unusually sluggish or sore, seek veterinary advice.

Attempts to pull a tick free will invariably leave the headpart in the pup, where it will die and cause an infected wound or abscess. The best way to remove ticks is to dab a strong saline solution, iodine, or alcohol on them. This will numb them, causing them to loosen their hold, at which time they can be removed with forceps. The wound can then be cleaned and covered with an antiseptic ointment. If ticks are common in your area, consult with your vet for a suitable pesticide to be used in kennels, on bedding, and on the puppy or dog.

INSECTS AND OTHER OUTDOOR DANGERS

There are many biting insects, such as mosquitoes, that can cause discomfort to a puppy. Many diseases are transmitted by the males of these species.

A pup can easily get a grass seed or thorn lodged between his pads or in the folds of his ears. These may go unnoticed until an abscess forms.

This is where your daily check of the puppy or dog will do a world of good. If your puppy has been playing in long grass or places where there may be thorns, pine needles, wild animals, or parasites, the checkup is a wise precaution.

SKIN DISORDERS

Apart from problems associated with lesions created by biting pests, a puppy may fall foul to a number of other skin disorders. Examples are ringworm, mange, and eczema. Ringworm is not caused by a worm, but is a fungal infection. It manifests itself as a sore-looking bald circle. If your puppy should have any form of bald patches, let your veterinarian check him over; a microscopic examination can confirm the condition. Many old remedies for ringworm exist, such as iodine, carbolic acid, formalin, and other tinctures, but modern drugs are superior.

Fungal infections can be very difficult to treat, and even more difficult to eradicate, because of the spores. These can withstand most treatments, other than burning, which is the best thing to do with bedding once the condition has been confirmed.

Mange is a general term that can be applied to many skin conditions where the hair falls out and a flaky crust develops and falls away.

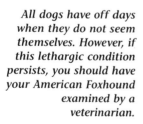

All dogs have off days when they do not seem themselves. However, if this lethargic condition persists, you should have your American Foxhound examined by a veterinarian.

Often, dogs will scratch themselves, and this invariably is worse than the original condition, for it opens lesions that are then subject to viral, fungal, or parasitic attack. The cause of the problem can be various species of mites. These either live on skin debris and the hair follicles, which they destroy, or they bury themselves just beneath the skin and feed on the tissue. Applying general remedies from pet stores is not recommended because it is essential to identify the type of mange before a specific treatment is effective.

Eczema is another non-specific term applied to many skin disorders. The condition can be brought about in many ways. Sunburn, chemicals, allergies to foods, drugs, pollens, and even stress can all produce a deterioration of the skin and coat. Given the range of causal factors, treatment can be difficult because the problem is one of identification. It is a case of taking each possibility at a time and trying to correctly diagnose the matter. If the cause is of a dietary nature then you must remove one item at a time in order to find out if the dog is allergic to a given food. It could, of course, be the lack of a nutrient that is the problem, so if the condition persists, you should consult your veterinarian.

INTERNAL DISORDERS

It cannot be overstressed that it is very foolish to attempt to diagnose an internal disorder without the advice of a veterinarian. Take a relatively common problem such as diarrhea. It might be caused by nothing more serious than the puppy hogging a lot of food or eating something that it has never previously eaten. Conversely, it could be the first indication of a potentially fatal disease. It's up to your veterinarian to make the correct diagnosis.

The following symptoms, especially if they accompany each other or are progressively added to earlier symptoms, mean you should visit the veterinarian right away:

Continual vomiting. All dogs vomit from time to time and this is not necessarily a sign of illness. They will eat grass to induce vomiting. It is a natural cleansing process common to many carnivores. However, continued vomiting is a clear sign of a problem. It may be a blockage in the pup's intestinal tract, it may be induced by worms, or it could be due to any number of diseases.

Diarrhea. This, too, may be nothing more than a temporary condition due to many factors. Even a change of home can induce diarrhea, because this often stresses the pup, and invariably there is some change in the diet. If it persists more than 48 hours then something is amiss. If blood is seen in the feces, waste no time at all in taking the dog to the vet.

Running eyes and/or nose. A pup might have a chill and this will cause the eyes and nose to weep. Again, this should quickly clear up if the puppy is placed in a warm environment and away from any drafts. If it does not, and especially if a mucous discharge is seen, then the pup has an illness that must be diagnosed.

Coughing. Prolonged coughing is a sign of a problem, usually of a respiratory nature.

Wheezing. If the pup has difficulty breathing and makes a wheezing sound when breathing, then something is wrong.

Cries when attempting to defecate or urinate. This might only be a minor problem due to the hard state of the feces, but it could be more serious, especially if the pup cries when urinating.

Cries when touched. Obviously, if you do not handle a puppy with care he might yelp. However, if he cries even when lifted gently, then he has an internal problem that becomes apparent when pressure is applied to a given area of the body. Clearly, this must be diagnosed.

Refuses food. Generally, puppies and dogs are greedy creatures when it comes to feeding time. Some might be more fussy, but none should refuse more than one meal. If they go for a number of hours without showing any interest in their food, then something is not as it should be.

General listlessness. All puppies have their off days when they do not seem their usual cheeky, mischievous selves. If this condition persists for more than two days then there is little doubt of a problem. They may not show any of the signs listed, other than perhaps a reduced interest in their food. There are many diseases that can develop internally without displaying obvious clinical signs. Blood, fecal, and other tests are needed in order to identify the disorder before it reaches an advanced state that may not be treatable.

WORMS

There are many species of worms, and a number of these live in the tissues of dogs and most other animals. Many create no problem at all, so you are not even aware they exist. Others can be tolerated in small levels, but become a major problem if they number more than a few. The most common types seen in dogs are roundworms and tapeworms. While roundworms are the greater problem, tapeworms require an intermediate host so are more easily eradicated.

Roundworms of the species Toxocara canis infest the dog. They may grow to a length of 8 inches (20 cm) and look like strings of spaghetti. The worms feed on the digesting food in the pup's intestines. In chronic cases the puppy will become pot-bellied, have diarrhea, and will vomit. Eventually, he will stop eating, having passed through the stage when he always seems hungry. The worms lay eggs in the puppy and these pass out in his feces. They are then either ingested by the pup, or they are eaten by mice, rats, or beetles. These may then be eaten by the puppy and the life cycle is complete.

Larval worms can migrate to the womb of a pregnant bitch, or to her mammary glands, and this is how they pass to the puppy. The pregnant bitch can be wormed, which will help. The pups can, and should, be wormed when they are about two weeks old. Repeat worming every 10 to 14 days and the parasites should be removed. Worms can be extremely dangerous to young puppies, so you should be sure the pup is wormed as a matter of routine.

Tapeworms can be seen as tiny rice-like eggs sticking to the puppy's or dog's anus. They are less destructive, but still undesirable. The eggs are eaten by mice, fleas, rabbits, and other animals that serve as intermediate hosts. They develop into a larval stage and the host must be eaten by the dog in order to complete the chain. Your vet will supply a suitable remedy if tapeworms are seen or suspected. There are other worms, such as hookworms and whipworms, that are also blood suckers. They will make a pup anemic, and blood might be

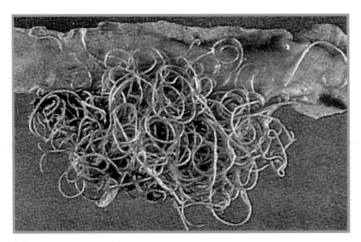

Roundworms are spaghetti-like worms that cause a pot-bellied appearance and dull coat, along with more severe symptoms, such as diarrhea and vomiting. Photo courtesy of Merck AgVet.

Whipworms are hard to find unless you strain your dog's feces, and this is best left to your veterinarian. Pictured here are adult whipworms.

seen in the feces, which can be examined by the vet to confirm their presence. Cleanliness in all matters is the best preventative measure for all worms.

Heartworm infestation in dogs is passed by mosquitoes but can be prevented by a monthly (or daily) treatment that is given orally. Talk to your vet about the risk of heartworm in your area.

BLOAT (GASTRIC DILATATION)

This condition has proved fatal in many dogs, especially large and deep-chested breeds, such as the Weimaraner and the Great Dane. However, any dog can get bloat. It is caused by swallowing air during exercise, food/water gulping or another strenuous task. As many believe, it is not the result of flatulence. The stomach of an affected dog twists, disallowing food and blood flow and resulting in harmful toxins being released into the bloodstream. Death can easily follow if the condition goes undetected.

The best preventative measure is not to feed large meals or exercise your puppy or dog immediately after he has eaten. Veterinarians recommend feeding three smaller meals per day in an elevated feeding rack, adding water to dry food to prevent gulping, and not offering water during mealtimes.

VACCINATIONS

Every puppy, purebred or mixed breed, should be vaccinated against the major canine diseases. These are distemper, leptospirosis, hepatitis, and canine parvovirus. Your puppy may have received a temporary vaccination against distemper before you purchased him, but get a copy of his health records from the breeder to be sure.

The age at which vaccinations are given can vary, but will usually be when the pup is 8 to 12 weeks old. By this time any protection given to the pup by antibodies received from his mother via her initial milk feeds will be losing their strength.

The puppy's immune system works on the basis that the white blood cells engulf and render harmless attacking bacteria. However, they must first recognize a potential enemy.

Vaccines are either dead bacteria or they are live, but in very small doses. Either type prompts the pup's defense system to attack them. When a large attack then comes (if it does), the immune system recognizes it and massive numbers of lymphocytes (white blood corpuscles) are mobilized to counter the attack. However, the ability of the cells to recognize these dangerous viruses can diminish over a period of time. It is therefore useful to provide annual reminders about the

Regular physical examinations are vital to the health and long life of your canine companion.

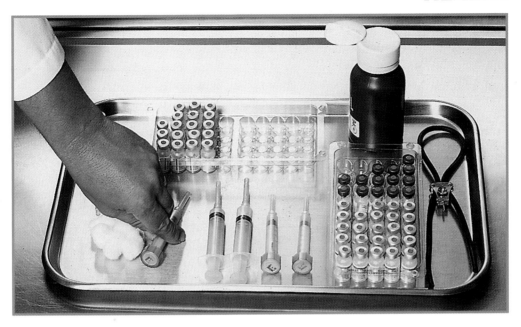

nature of the enemy. This is done by means of booster injections that keep the immune system on its alert. Immunization is not 100-percent guaranteed to be successful, but is very close. Certainly it is better than giving the puppy no protection.

Dogs are subject to other viral attacks, and if these are of a high-risk factor in your area, then your vet will suggest you have the puppy vaccinated against these as well.

Your puppy or dog should also be vaccinated against the deadly rabies virus. In fact, in many places it is illegal for your dog not to be vaccinated. This is to protect your dog, your family, and the rest of the animal population from this deadly virus that infects the nervous system and causes dementia and death.

ACCIDENTS

All puppies will get their share of bumps and bruises due to the rather energetic way they play. These will usually heal themselves over a few days. Small cuts should be bathed with a suitable disinfectant and then smeared with an antiseptic ointment. If a cut looks more serious, then stem the flow of blood with a towel or makeshift tourniquet and rush the pup to the veterinarian. Never apply so much pressure to the wound that it might restrict the flow of blood to the limb.

In the case of burns you should apply cold water or an ice pack to the surface. If the burn was due to a chemical, then this must be washed away with copious

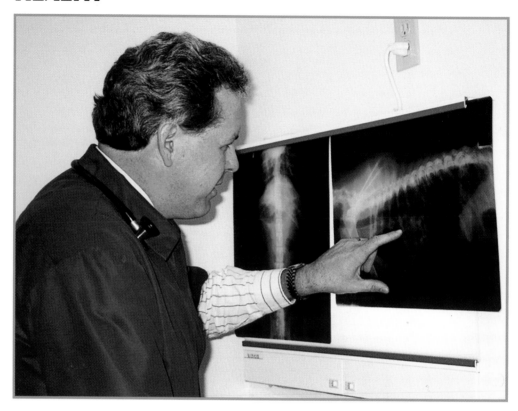

amounts of water. Apply petroleum jelly, or any vegetable oil, to the burn. Trim away the hair if need be. Wrap the dog in a blanket and rush him to the vet. The pup may go into shock, depending on the severity of the burn, and this will result in a lowered blood pressure, which is dangerous and the reason the pup must receive immediate veterinary attention.

If a broken limb is suspected then try to keep the animal as still as possible. Wrap your pup or dog in a blanket to restrict movement and get him to the veterinarian as soon as possible. Do not move the dog's head so it is tilting backward, as this might result in blood entering the lungs.

Do not let your pup jump up and down from heights, as this can cause considerable shock to the joints. Like all youngsters, puppies do not know when enough is enough, so you must do all their thinking for them.

Provided you apply strict hygiene to all aspects of raising your puppy, and you make daily checks on his physical state, you have done as much as you can to safeguard him during his most vulnerable period. Routine visits to your veterinarian are also recommended, especially while the puppy is under one year of age.

If your American Foxhound becomes ill or sustains an injury from an accident or fall, acting quickly and appropriately can save his life. For example, it is a good idea to x-ray any dog hit by a car.

Opposite: Your American Foxhound will be a valued member of the family for a long time, so you'll want to ensure that he enjoys good health and a quality lifestyle. Stuart Smith and Ch. Vaught's Hello Dolly.

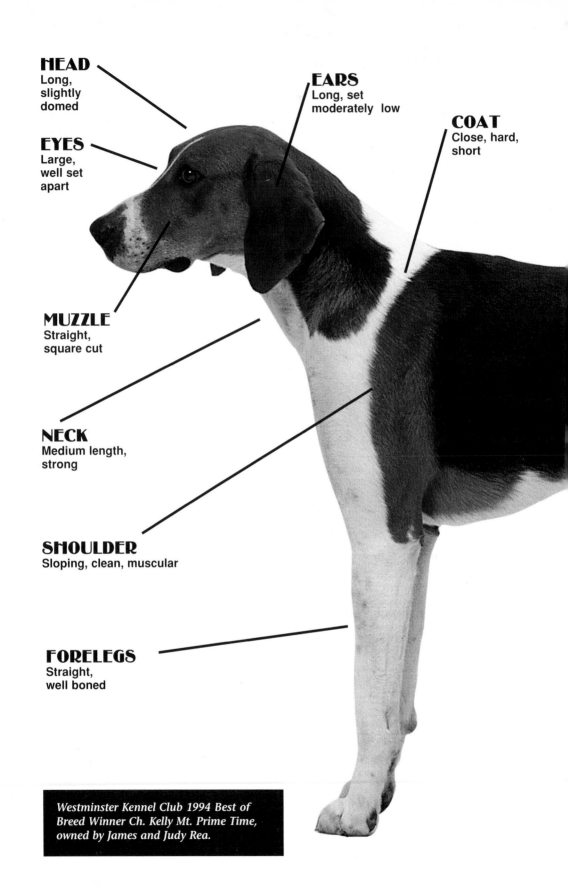

HEAD
Long,
slightly
domed

EARS
Long, set
moderately low

COAT
Close, hard,
short

EYES
Large,
well set
apart

MUZZLE
Straight,
square cut

NECK
Medium length,
strong

SHOULDER
Sloping, clean, muscular

FORELEGS
Straight,
well boned

*Westminster Kennel Club 1994 Best of
Breed Winner Ch. Kelly Mt. Prime Time,
owned by James and Judy Rea.*